Gary Collins

Successful
Selling

In easy steps is an imprint of In Easy Steps Limited
4 Chapel Court · 42 Holly Walk · Leamington Spa
Warwickshire · United Kingdom · CV32 4YS
www.ineasysteps.com

Notice of Liability
Every effort has been made to ensure that this book contains accurate
and current information. However, In Easy Steps Limited and the
author shall not be liable for any loss or damage suffered by readers
as a result of any information contained herein.

Trademarks
All trademarks are acknowledged as belonging to their respective
companies.

In Easy Steps Limited supports The Forest Stewardship Council (FSC),
the leading international forest certification organisation. All our titles
that are printed on Greenpeace approved FSC certified paper carry the
FSC logo.

MIX
Paper from
responsible sources
FSC® C020837

Printed and bound in the United Kingdom

ISBN 978-1-84078-424-4

Contents

1

Getting Started

"It is our attitude at the beginning of a difficult undertaking that, more than anything else, will determine its successful outcome."

William James

Introduction

"You can learn new things at any time in your life if you're willing to be a beginner. If you actually learn to like being a beginner, the whole world opens up to you." – Barbara Sher

When I began to think about what this book should contain, in order to make it as useful as possible, I reflected on the numerous books I have read on sales techniques, most of which seem to have been written by academics.

Naturally, those authors have never been in Sales and, of course, can have a good idea about the theory of the Sales process, but I feel that an author's long and successful experience in numerous selling roles is more likely to make a book's contents useful to the reader.

This is written from a background of real experiences and situations that have led, through those experiences, to pragmatic learning and development. I have, of course, made mistakes along the way and, by talking about the lessons learned, I intend to give you the opportunity to shortcut that learning process. Why should you have to repeat the mistakes that I have made just to understand that you need to do things in a different way?

With that in mind, I have written this book in a way that I believe will give you genuine helpful, informative and practical tips to help you become more successful in your Sales career.

You can try these ideas and methods immediately and see the benefits they bring in real terms – more customer meetings, better information gathering, winning propositions, more orders and, therefore, a greater Sales performance.

Each element of the sales process is covered in simple categories, so you can easily find what you need for any given circumstance.

Like so many things in our lives, sales is a process that can be broken down into a series of steps, each of which is covered in order. Helping you find the actions and style that will suit you and what will help you succeed. The only thing that you need to do is try them, learn them and use them.

For the newcomer, I will help you get into the sales process without forming bad habits, which will become difficult to change once they are ingrained into your performance and style.

For the experienced Sales person, I will give you enough tips and ideas so that you will find something you hadn't previously thought of, or which will act as a reminder about something you are currently no longer doing.

It is so easy for us to get into a rhythm in our techniques and not have the opportunity to review them. This prevents us making the necessary adjustments that will increase our productivity.

This book will act as a prompt so that you revisit your own techniques as well as discovering some new ones. As with bad ones, getting into good habits can easily be achieved and doing the right things at the right time will soon become natural, automatic and successful.

For this title to be genuinely comprehensive, it would need to be in several volumes. As I don't have that luxury, I have covered those issues I know are fundamental to you being successful in your Sales career.

The fundamental element of what we need to do in a Sales role is to uncover and create "needs" and "wants" your Prospect (or customer) has. We need to understand what their key drivers and motivations are and then have the ability to be creative enough to find a solution to those issues.

This book will often save you the "creative" bit but, if it doesn't, you may well have the answer based on your own experiences; you sometimes simply need to take a step back, think about your other experiences with similar customer types and, consequently, relate the solutions to what you face now.

You will also be surrounded by colleagues who will also have knowledge and experiences to draw on, too, so make sure that, if you uncover a situation you are finding difficult to handle, you seek help and advice from those around you. Never be afraid to ask for help and guidance – the only stupid question is the one you don't ask.

A critical aspect of your organization's continued success, especially within challenging markets, will be the ability of its external salespeople to protect and increase profitable business with current customers, whilst winning business from new ones.

...cont'd

Strengthening the skills required to consistently achieve those outcomes is the focus of this book.

A key player in your success should be your Sales Manager. One of my most disappointing discoveries in recent years is that Sales Managers no longer seem to coach and guide their sales teams, which I believe should be fundamental in what they do. Instead, it appears that they give them challenging targets and chastise them for not achieving them, rather than helping them achieve them.

They will find time in their busy day to chase their Sales people for not doing their reports on time (which I accept is an important element of the whole Sales process) but they rarely seem to do the most fundamental task I believe they are employed to do. Being an excellent Sales coach, to ensure that every one of their Sales team is operating at the very highest level of their ability and productivity, would be the most productive and effective use of their time and position and would produce the best possible results for their Sales Teams, themselves and their organizations.

They have the opportunity to observe you in action, take an objective view and, therefore, help you adjust your style to maximize your success.

My aim is to become your 'virtual' Sales Manager, someone who can coach and help you be the very best Sales Person you can be.

*If you are a **Sales Manager** reading this book, I ask you to reflect on your own activity and motivations. Are you helping your team to improve and develop by using your own experiences, knowledge and skills? If you are not, what could you do to change that situation? Do you have the coaching skills to carry out that element of your role and, if not, how can you improve to become an excellent Sales coach? Your role is to achieve targets and objectives through the performance of the individuals who report to you; the better you can make them, the more success you will have yourself. My experience as a Salesman, Regional Sales Manager and Head of Sales is that help and support is more effective than punishment and penalty.*

I hope that you will take this book with you as you travel, so that, before you go into your Sales call, you will review your meeting objectives and remind yourself of some ideas on how you can ensure that you meet those objectives. Working in Sales is a very rewarding and enjoyable career – as long as you are successful. To a degree, you are your own boss, with the flexibility to decide who you see and when you see them. The contents of this book will help you in your productivity, effectiveness and success so that you really can enjoy your Sales career.

Some basics

Be an optimist

There are some fundamental things you should know - if you don't already - about your life in Sales.

The first thing I need to tell you is that this career is one that will only suit you if you are an optimist; someone with an energy and drive to accomplish their goals. You will spend many days alone between sales calls, which, day after day, can be very difficult.

Despite your contact with customers and 'the office', you are primarily alone in terms of motivation and handling difficult issues.

- It's YOU who has to decide whether to get out of bed in the morning and walk into that first sales call

- It's YOU who decides which direction to steer your car as you drive away from your home

- It's YOU who decides what your day's objectives are

For that reason, Attitude plays a huge part in your ability to succeed. I think it's crucial and want to give you some sporting examples of why I believe that to be true.

The 4-minute mile

Break through barriers

On 6 May 1954, Roger Bannister became the first man in history to run the mile in under four minutes. He ran the distance in 3 minutes 59.4 seconds. Apart from the fact that, in doing so, he broke the world record for the mile, Bannister's feat was even more remarkable when you look at the thinking of the era, especially amongst those in the medical profession.

At that time, it was believed that running that fast over that distance was physically impossible. The heart was thought unable to pump blood around the body fast enough to fuel the muscles with sufficient oxygen to perform to that high a level. Roger Bannister, however, didn't believe them – he believed that he could run that fast and so it proved.

I think this is a perfect example of how your attitude to a task can have such a demonstrable impact on the outcome.

Maybe what supports my thinking even more is that I was not surprised to learn that, having spent over 2000 years not running that fast because we didn't believe that human beings could, it took just 46 days for another athlete to not only break the 4-minute mile but Roger Bannister's newly set record. John Landy of Australia ran the mile in 3 minutes 58.0 seconds.

Once it was believed and even accepted that it was possible, others achieved the same feat. Today, the mile has been completed in less than four minutes over 4500 times by almost 1000 athletes

...cont'd

with the current record, set by El Guerrouj in 1999, at 3 minutes 43.13 seconds.

There is no doubt that technology and sports science have played their part in that significant reduction in time, with the production of better track surfaces and better running shoes and diet knowledge. However, I still believe that attitude was significant for the current situation in World athletics. I wonder if anyone will ever have the belief that El Guerrouj's record will one day be broken.

Achieve the impossible

The second example is even more astonishing.

You may even think that I have embellished this story as you read on; I haven't and I strongly advise you to use your favored search engine to find out more about this incredible man.

The man is called Cliff Young, he was an Australian sheep farmer. In the early 1980's, he ran a 2000 acre sheep farm with his 81-year-old mother. They had 2000 sheep but could not afford a vehicle to get around the farm to round them up when the storms came in. So Cliff Young would run around his 2000 acres to herd the sheep and bring them in. Now that's not the remarkable bit, although, in itself, it is an impressive feat.

In 1981, when Cliff was 63, he decided to enter the 'Sydney to Melbourne' Ultra Marathon. Standard Marathons are impressive enough, especially when taking into account the time taken to run them by today's top athletes. However, running an Ultra Marathon is astonishing. This Ultra Marathon was 544 miles long.

Cliff Young turned up at the start to collect his race number and was greeted with disbelief when he told the stewards that he was there to compete.

The thing is, there's more to this remarkable story than first meets the eye. Whilst the other highly toned athletes had the very latest equipment – Lycra® running clothes, bespoke running shoes, etc., Cliff turned up in overalls and galoshes!

The other thing that all the other athletes had was a support vehicle; a camper van where they could rest. The known wisdom of Ultra Marathons was that you ran for 18 hours and slept for 6 hours. Cliff didn't have a van or anywhere else that he could rest.

The race started and the other athletes soon began to lose Cliff as he shuffled along, losing ground. He didn't have the best of knees so instead of striding out like Michael Johnson, he kind of shuffled along, with just short strides, not bending his knees much to maintain a low impact style for his ailing knees.

The main group was well ahead of him by the time nightfall came and they stopped for their sleep and recuperation. Cliff Young didn't realize that you were supposed to stop to rest... so he didn't; he just kept on running through the night. This went on for 4 days and 4 nights. He just kept on running.

During the 5th night, he caught up with the other athletes and overtook them, winning the race and breaking the previous record by over 9 hours. He later explained that, as he was running, he imagined chasing sheep as a storm rolled in off the mountains.

You must believe in yourself

The point is, his superhuman feat was achieved because his attitude was one of pure self-belief. He believed that he could run for over 5 days and nights without stopping to rest. So he did.

Just think how powerful that attitude could be in other areas of life – and specifically in your sales career.

Every single very successful sales person I have ever had the pleasure to work with has had a similar attitude, that no matter how tough their targets were, they believed they could achieve them, and, of course, they invariably did.

Look around you at your colleagues and you will recognize that

- some spend their time explaining that their targets are unachievable, and

- others just get on with things

Invariably, both achieve what they expect to achieve.

Don't forget

Have great attitude and believe you can achieve your goals. Only those that believe will consistently succeed.

1 Remember Cliff Young when you feel that the task ahead of you is a daunting one

2 Decide to take the approach that you can conquer it

3 Then make sure that you do.

The rewards and satisfaction will make the effort worthwhile – every time.

Be driven and self-motivated

Communication is certainly easier and faster now than it has ever been, with the development of excellent new technology tools.

However, you will still inevitably have days when nothing seems to go right and there isn't someone sitting next to you to chat with or discuss last night's TV to get your mind off the difficult day you're having. So you must be someone with

- optimism
- drive
- a real desire to succeed.

Without these qualities, you can still have a career in Sales but I would doubt very much that it would be either enjoyable or successful.

I feel that there is a comparison to be made with a Sports career; a top athlete or sports star will be able to

- pick themselves up when things go wrong
- try a new tactic when the current one isn't working, and
- drive on through adversity to ensure they have done everything in their power to succeed.

So, if you are the sort of person who likes a challenge and has a competitive streak, welcome to your successful sales career – I hope it's a long and successful one.

If you're not, maybe you should evaluate your choice of career and take a look at something else; in the long run, it may well be the best thing to do.

In summary, performance can be described easily as a simply equation:

P = A + A   (Performance = Ability + Attitude)

Summary

- Be an optimist – selling can be a lonely profession; you need to be positive about what you can achieve and keep your enthusiasm up, even during difficult days

- Anything is possible if you have the right motivation and truly believe you can achieve it. You are the one who will set your own boundaries – make sure they are wide enough to achieve your objectives

- Remember Cliff Young – have a reminder for yourself that simply says "Cliff Young Thinking" to focus your mind on your high level goals – then make sure you achieve them

- Motivation comes from within you. It is not your manager's responsibility to get you motivated to be successful; it's yours

- Keep your energy levels high, to enable you to be involved in the right activities, which will deliver your success

- Set regular goals for yourself – specific achievements that, together, will deliver your overall objectives

2

Planning

Using time effectively

How much time do we really have?

The first thing you have to take into account, when you start to plan how you will achieve your targets and objectives, is to consider what resource you have available to you.

The prominent resource you have is yourself – or to be more specific, your available time; that is your sales currency. If you haven't considered this so far, you might be surprised to know that you will typically have only 141 days available to you for face to face customer meetings out of the 365 in the full year. By the time you have taken out holidays, weekends, conferences and meetings, training and sickness, you are likely to lose over 200 days. On the face of it that sounds unlikely, so it's worth analyzing why that's the case.

Typical time stealers are:

Holidays	42
Weekends	104
Bank Holidays	8
Sales Meetings	12
Conferences	2
Training	6
Sickness	4
Planning and admin	46
Total lost	**224**

Be efficient with your time

Taking that into account, it emphasizes why it is critical that you use those available days as effectively and productively as possible. It also demonstrates why your territory planning (route planning) needs to be tight and efficient. Many sales people don't actually have a route plan, which means that they spend those precious available days in ad hoc activities, reacting to issues that happen and are considered important or urgent by others rather than themselves. It is vital that you have control of your own time; make it full of activity, which is going to ensure that you reach your goals – often short term – which leads to the achievement of your longer term objectives.

Hot tip

Ensure you use your scarce sales time productively. You lose over 50% of total days each year in other activity, so you have to be smart in how you use your time.

Beware time stealers

The loss of quality customer facing time doesn't stop with the "stealers" mentioned above. In fact, they are merely the start and, are primarily out of your control. You can be your worst enemy if you do not ensure that you avoid losing many more hours and days with typical time wasters, such as:

- Leaving home late – returning home early

- Not arranging the first appointment until 10.00 am

- Calling to show, demonstrate and sell products without sufficient preparation

- Using the telephone inefficiently

- Not using the planning day effectively

- Inappropriately long business lunches

- Meeting with people who cannot influence the sale

- Writing unnecessarily detailed reports during sales time, rather than out of business hours

- Over-calling on regular customers

- Unnecessary visits to company locations during selling time to collect literature, samples, etc

- Unnecessary waiting at a customer's premises because an appointment was not made

- Bad route planning and failure to plan movements

- Wasting time and effort on those customers whose potential is limited

- Waiting at home for the morning post before setting out

- Failure to prepare for each customer meeting

- Failure to contact the right decision maker

Route planning

Plan your routes efficiently so you cover all relevant parts of your territory regularly, which will lead to effective time management.

Take control

Maintaining that control means that the only person who can strongly influence your end result is you, which is how it should be.

That control means that you need to be assertive at times with those people who attempt to steal your time. Even customers should be told "no" when they demand unscheduled visits – invariably, the issue that they want to discuss with you will wait until the next time you are scheduled to be in their geographical area.

Don't be pressured into a complete re-schedule of your planning because somebody else shouts loud enough. It also means that you need to plan well, taking into account

1. where your key customers and prospects are, and

2. where your potential can be realized to meet those year-end targets.

A typical route plan will look like this:

	Monday	Tuesday	Wednesday	Thursday	Friday
Week 1	Zone 1	Zone 2	Zone 3	Zone 4	Planning
Week 2	Zone 5	Zone 6	Free/ Flexible	Zone 7	Zone 1
Week 3	Zone 2	Zone 3	Planning	Zone 4	Zone 5
Week 4	Zone 6	Free/ Flexible	Zone 8	Sales Meeting	Zone 7

Regular route patterns

You will see that there is a regular pattern for your area visits, which means that it is easy for you to make your next meeting appointment while with your customer, rather than having to phone nearer the time to arrange something important.

The 'free' days are not actually free from work, of course; they give you the opportunity to fit something unexpected in at reasonably short notice or to use for that pro-active work you have been planning for quite some time.

Having a structured approach to your work schedule doesn't have to take away any flexibility that you might need.

Of course, you can change things around a little but do resist too much flexibility and change because that can easily lead to a totally ad hoc way of working, which will inevitably reduce your efficiency and effectiveness.

Beware

Don't lose productive time in your day by starting late and leaving your territory early.

When suits them?

Call at the right time

Some customers would prefer to see you at specific times of the day, to fit in with their own routine – if you do that, you immediately have them in a good mood; conversely, they are unlikely to give you their complete attention if you are interrupting their routine.

If they are relaxed about their own activity and time management, they are much more likely to listen and be receptive to what you are telling them.

As you get to know your customer and build a relationship, you will obviously know the best time to make your appointment, however, it's also very reasonable for you to ask that question when making the appointment with a new prospect.

This is particularly important with a Prospect because your intention is to create a very positive perception early in your business relationship. By fitting in with the customer's working day, you are much more likely to do just that.

The balance here is attempting to fit into your Prospect or Customer's day while also planning an efficient route to enable you to have a productive day.

Giving alternatives often works and also means that, to a large extent, you have control of the situation by offering them a choice that fits nicely into your day's schedule.

Creating your route plan

How should you create your route plan? What you shouldn't do is zigzag from one customer to another – criss-crossing across your geography and covering many more miles than you need to. Plan your route so that it:

- Flows in a nice efficient circle, if possible

- Leads you back home to your front door or office at the end of the working day

It's a good idea to have a map of your territory with each customer 'pinned' on it, to remind you of exactly where they are in relation to each other. This makes it much easier to plan your route effectively and efficiently.

Your journey plan should enable some flexibility to cater for unforeseen events or demands as well as putting you in each piece of your geography on a very regular basis.

If you need to have an amount of time in the office (or at home) each week or month to make appointments and complete administration, build that in too.

Hot tip

Plan well so that you can bring the future into the present to enable you to influence it.

Which companies?

Beware

It's very easy to get caught up with calling a prospect who doesn't offer realizable potential for you. You have to be disciplined and ruthless in account selection.

Who to call on

When you are building your Route Plan, you obviously need to take into account where the best potential and highest chance of success lies.

To truly plan your activity, you must spend some time evaluating the opportunities that lie within your area of responsibility. Once you have established where that opportunity exists, only then can you truly create a Route Plan that will deliver results.

There is a tried and tested formula I believe works very well and delivers what you need. You will require some customer information to use it, so, if you don't already have it, then that's your first activity determined.

To establish the right activity you need to be involved in you simply need to evaluate

1 all "value" opportunities that you have in combination

2 with your probability of success.

It is vital that you are not consumed with the overall potential a specific company has if your chances of converting that business is small.

The net result will almost certainly be failure to achieve sufficient volumes to reach your targets.

The other thing to bear in mind, of course, is that you need to "plan" for more than you need. Some potential that you feel sure will come in won't, as circumstances change; others will.

Either way, you need to have planned for that to ensure that you have more than you need rather than less.

Although this formula is very simple, it does work, as long as you have established two critical pieces of information:

1 What is the total available spend on your products or services

2 What is the percentage chance of success.

The latter will be based on

- your competitive position

- product value

- relationships

- brand strength

and all the other factors that influence a customer's decision to buy.

Do the maths!
This can look as simple as this:

Customer	Location	Potential Value	Success Probability	Realizable Value
Acme Trading	Zone 1	10,000	60%	6,000
Beta Manufacturing	Zone 3	30,000	25%	7,500
Gamma Distribution	Zone 7	8,000	100%	8,000
Delta & Co	Zone 7	25,000	80%	20,000
Collins Brothers Ltd	Zone 3	50,000	10%	5,000
A.B.C Corp	Zone 4	100,000	15%	15,000
Totals		*223,000*	*27.58%*	*61,500*

...cont'd

Calculating successful routes

This chart shows several things.

It demonstrates how easy it would be to follow the greatest volume, despite low chances of success.

In this example, although ABC Corp has the greatest overall potential value, the probability of success means that it will deliver less than Delta & Co.

It also shows that zone 4 has the greatest overall potential value but zone 7 is likely to yield the highest returns.

Naturally, the chart here is no more than an example and, for you to truly plan your activity effectively, you will need to include all known companies available to you with the relevant information.

Then simply filter with highest realizable value at the top of the table and plot your Route Planner around the companies and, therefore, the zones that will deliver the most.

That's where you need to be spending your time and that's how you will maximize your ability to be successful. This can be a time consuming exercise initially but will pay dividends through the year if created accurately.

Beware

Beware of unproductive customer meetings. Always set both primary and secondary objectives which support business growth as well as considering what the customer wants from your time together.

Controlling the customer meeting

Taking control of your time

It is, as mentioned, vital that you take and maintain control of what happens in your Sales activity.

That starts with your:

- time management

- planning, and

- the actual sales call itself

During that time in the call when you are asking questions, you are in control.

Make sure that, as much as is possible, you maintain that control throughout the call; including how much time you spend there.

The most successful and consistent salesman I ever worked with would always set himself a time limit for each call, based on his call objectives and the value/potential available.

He would then ensure that, subject to something extraordinary happening, he finished the meeting at the time that suited him.

He kept control and ensured that he didn't waste time by being a bad leaver (A bad leaver is simply what it says – someone who wants to get away from a situation but struggles to find the right way to do so.) This allowed him to keep his sales call rate up and improve his productivity.

Other communication methods

It is also important to understand that, as important as face to face customer meetings are, there are times when the communication needed can be by another means.

If a discussion is needed, you can consider a phone call of course. It may seem obvious, however, do not start the relationship building process with a telephone "meeting".

...cont'd

Once you have started getting to know your customer or prospect, you may need to ask or tell them a piece of information so then pick up the phone.

This activity can easily come into the area of "Comfort zone calling" where a Sales person convinces themselves that they need to make a customer meeting for a 5 minute conversation.

It's another call for the report sheet for that day but it's another time stealer when a phone conversation would have served the same purpose.

Avoid comfort calling

Comfort zone calling will also include those people that you know very well, and probably like, too, but who either do not have an application or need for your product or service, or, if they do, the potential is not at a sufficiently high level to warrant more than an occasional meeting.

Worse still, they may not have the necessary influence or authority to make a decision on whether you can do business together. If that's the case, recognize it early and spend your time with those who genuinely CAN influence your ability to achieve your goals and objectives.

You have no control of the relentless passing of time. However, you do have control on how you use the time available to you. Use it wisely and your chance of success is greatly increased.

One more sales call

That extra call

Even if you just work the numbers game, an extra good quality and well planned sales call each day has got to deliver improved results.

Just look at your normal conversion rate of 'calls to sale' and work out how much more business you could generate by being more efficient in each sales call and, therefore, having one more face-to-face with a customer or prospect each day.

Summary

- During the course of any given year, the time available for sales calls is diminished by holidays, meetings, planning and training. Therefore, you must use what's left effectively

- Make sure that you don't steal extra chunks from your sales time through inefficient activities, such as short days and inappropriate use of the telephone

- Route planning is critical in ensuring that you cover all customers and locations at an appropriate level, to maximize opportunities. Be disciplined with your route plan and build in days for flexibility and ad-hoc demands and opportunities

- To improve your chances of getting the quality customer meetings you need, carefully consider what days and times suit your customer contacts best

- Understand the difference between route planning and journey planning. To maximize your use of available selling time, create a journey plan that takes you on a natural circular route from and back to your base, whether it's your home or office

- Account selection is critical, to ensure that your chances of success are maximized. The largest isn't necessarily the best – take into account your competitive position, value and probability of success when prioritizing those customers who will deliver the largest returns

- The meetings that you have with your customers and prospects need to be structured, controlled and effective. Plan thoroughly and know exactly what information you need to gather, as well as identifying your primary and secondary objectives ,before you start

- Your productivity will increase by 15-20% simply by getting one more call into each working day

3

Prospecting

"Sales are contingent upon the attitude of the salesman - not the attitude of the prospect."

- W. Clement Stone

Which companies?

Clearly you have to find out exactly who your potential customers are in your attempt to grow your business. You then have to decide how to approach them and what your proposition will be.

This can be either difficult or easy, depending on how you decide to approach it. I am not trying to suggest that the whole area of prospecting is easy – your success, however, will largely be determined by the amount of thought and effort you put into it.

Do enough prospecting

The first thing you should realize is that today's prospects are tomorrow's loyal customers. I know that, for many of you, this will seem like a completely obvious statement, but not every sales person seems to realize it.

Without putting the right amount of effort and thought into your prospecting activity, the likelihood is that your attempts to reach sales targets year after year will not be successful. Therefore, your planning time needs to include activities for both new and existing customers.

The key point I'm trying to convey to you is simply that, if you don't make contact with them to enable you to present your proposition, they will never be customers.

Ratios

The definition of ratio is "the relationship between two numbers or amounts expressed as a proportion." - Collins English Dictionary.

Know our ratios

In many ways, every aspect of our lives works on ratios. What this means is that there are relationships between different activities, which you need to understand to ensure that you spend your time doing the right things in the right volumes to ensure successful outcomes. We all have our own ratios and you need to know what yours are.

Most companies will have a set of financial ratios, which enables them to judge their overall performance and consequently make good quality decisions. As a Sales Professional, you need to know several sets of ratios in order to maximize your success. These are likely to be things like:

- Average success rate of the performance of your product against your competition

- Average number of telephone calls needed to gain an appointment

- Average number of appointments needed to gain time to 'pitch'

- Average number of pitches needed to take an order

- Average value of new customer

Using these numbers to plan your activity will enable you to schedule enough telephone calls and, subsequently, book enough customer appointments to achieve your goals. Let's look at an example.

On average, you might need to make five telephone calls to gain one appointment from a prospect. Your conversion rate of prospect calls to new customer might be one in four. Your Sales Manager then gives you a target of gaining 25 new customers in the given year. This is when your ratios kick in.

Calculate your ratios and use them to manage your activity, to ensure you maximize the chances of hitting your objectives.

...cont'd

You need to plan enough activity

Achieving 25 new customers requires 100 prospect calls, which require 500 prospect telephone calls. Taking an average year, with 46 working weeks, you need to make approximately 11 prospect telephone calls per week or roughly 2 per day.

Once you know that, you can then plan it and make sure it happens. When you break something down into activity per day, it really does put it into perspective and, in this example, two prospect phone calls per day is fairly minimal in terms of effort, it will however maximize your chances of success.

If you don't, that chance of success is greatly reduced. So even if the numbers come out at a rather frightening level, make sure you work them out – you need to know what it's going to take to achieve your targets.

First steps

Sources of information

So how do you find out who those potential customers are?

If you are fortunate enough, your company may have or buy a database with prospect lists you can use. You may even be able to get someone else to qualify it for you – to cut out the companies that are no longer in existence.

Even if you do have access to such a great tool, you should also look to find your own new prospects. The important thing to realize is that there are many opportunities for you to find prospects, some of whom will turn into important and loyal customers.

Take a look around

Be observant

Every day, in all that you do, you have the opportunity to seek out more prospects.

It starts when you leave your home and drive to your first meeting. There is absolutely no doubt whatsoever that, during that journey, you will pass many prospect opportunities. Keep your eyes open for company premises, sign-written commercial vehicles and billboard advertisements for companies that might have a need for your product or service.

While it's clearly vital that you concentrate on driving safely and courteously, that doesn't prevent you from noticing company names that you can remember and note down at a suitable moment.

In these days of internet search engines, information gathering has become so easy, a name is often all you need.

Local and commercial radio offers another good source of information. The advertisements you will hear are obviously created to generate new customers for the advertisers themselves, however, their very presence also alerts you to them as potential customers.

Use your contacts

Existing contacts

Your own customers can also be a source of prospects. Do be careful who and how you ask, because this could be a situation where their own competitors are a very sensitive subject of discussion for that customer.

However, there might well be other companies that your contact knows about who they feel would enjoy the benefits of your product or service, without being a threat to their own competitive position.

If you have been effective enough to have already built very good relationships with that customer, they may even make an introduction for you – and those are the very best types of prospects to have.

Hot tip

Get warm introductions whenever you can. These are much easier to convert and come with built in testimonials, simply because you've been introduced.

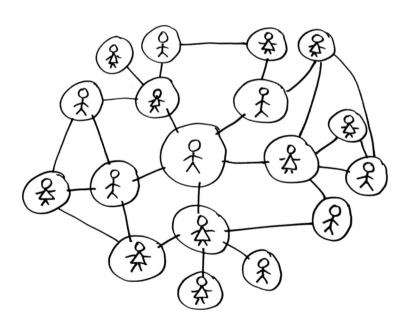

Who else can help?

Hot tip

The use of business networking sites can drastically improve your chances of getting in front of the right people, with the minimum of time and effort. By being members of these sites, people are announcing that they want to make new contacts.

Personal referrals

The same is true of suppliers. Some sales organizations work closely with other supplier sales personnel. These are usually third party suppliers – distributors or wholesalers.

If you are a sales person for these third party organizations, work your contacts. The supplier sales representatives will have built their own relationships with people who could become your customers, too.

In the right circumstances, that supplier may even be prepared to make a first-hand introduction for you – walk you in to see their contact in a dual customer meeting. These really are both very powerful and very valuable because someone the prospect trusts is introducing you into their organization. That gives you immediate credibility and a prospect that is listening to you and, open to your proposition.

My most successful Distributor relationship worked simply because the salesman concerned took me into all of his existing customers who may have had an application for my product (so I benefited) and I converted many of them to buy my product through his company (so he benefited). This type of working relationship can bring huge dividends, as well as making the whole area of gaining new customers so much more enjoyable.

How to make contact

The best approach

Now you have to decide how to approach them. As a simple rule of thumb, I would say that, unless all else has failed, you should never cold call – turning up at the premises without an appointment. Even if you have time on your hands and have found a prospect nearby, by all means drop in but only to get a few details from the receptionist about whom you should make contact with.

You might be lucky to get to see the right person but, in these days of busy people and tight schedules, it's very unlikely. It is also likely to create a negative perception for the company contact, that you would turn up out of the blue and hope to be seen.

Those days are gone and your initial contact should be through a well planned telephone call – assuming you can't get a third party introduction. So use the visit to simply gain information and set aside time to telephone your prospects to make an appointment.

This is not simply a matter of politeness; prospects will be much more willing to listen attentively to your proposition if it is delivered during an arranged time.

If by chance you did get to see your contact on an ad hoc call, the prospect is unlikely to be able to give you enough time to pay suitable attention to you, and you, therefore, run the risk of them making a snap judgement on your proposition simply through a rushed decision.

Internet networking

Another benefit of today's technology and communication channels is the creation and use of business networking sites.

The most popular one that I'm aware of is www.linkedIn.com. Literally millions of business people around the world have signed up to that site and have created a network of valuable contacts who they feel may be helpful to them at some point in the future.

It has many advantages, not least of which is the fact that, simply by creating their profile, they are demonstrating that they are open to contact and "linking" with other like-minded people. It also has the useful function of being a search engine in its own right for either companies or individuals. Therefore, if you have a company

...cont'd

name, you can search for all employees of that organization who have created their own profile page.

You might just find exactly the right person to make contact with and can then send a request to connect. They are on the site because they believe in its value, which means they are almost certain to agree to your request. Now you have made contact with someone who can help you achieve your objectives and goals and you have not had to resort to Cold Calling or even prospect telephone calls.

It is a very valuable tool and one that could save you hours of precious time uncovering key people in those companies you feel have the potential for a productive trading relationship.

Don't underestimate the power of these sites; it is how business people are choosing to make contact with valuable contacts and, if you are not part of it, you run the risk of allowing your competitors easy access to not only your prospects but your customers, too.

Booking sales calls

Phoning for appointments

As part of your planning activity, you have already established that you should be spending some time making telephone calls to book customer appointments.

Like all of your productive and effective sales activity, the telephone calls that you will make to set up customer meetings need to be planned and prepared for, so that you are ready for every eventuality.

When you make these telephone calls to prospects, your objective should be no more than to gain their commitment to a meeting.

Be careful not to get involved in selling over the phone. That can happen all too easily as you are very likely to be asked:

● "Why should I spend time listening to you?

● What are you going to offer me?"

This is where you have to have the ability to be able to give enough information to gain interest in a meeting but not enough for the contact to make a decision about your proposition on the spot.

Getting past the Gatekeeper

This activity has an added difficulty at times because most people you want to make contact with have someone between you and them whose sole purpose in life is to keep you apart – the "Gatekeeper".

They might be the telephonist, receptionist, secretary or P.A. or simply a colleague of that contact you wish to speak to. So how do you get past that gatekeeper?

Hot tip

Develop strong "hook" statements to gain immediate interest when speaking to prospects on the phone. You need them to see "value" in giving you their time.

43

Beware

Beware of the gatekeepers who will attempt to protect their colleagues from you. Speak confidently and assertively to get connected to your key contact.

Hot tip

Time your prospect phone calls for when your chances of getting through are highest. Early afternoon is often good, when the early rush is over and the end of day panic is yet to arrive.

...cont'd

Be assertive

The first thing that you need to do is use assertive behavior – ask to be put through without sounding as if it would be a huge favor for them to do so.

For you to do this effectively, you need to know the name of the person you want to speak to; asking for "the buyer" or "whoever is responsible for specifying which widget you use" immediately tells the other person that you have no relationship and are trying to sell something.

They will almost definitely become defensive at this point and not cooperate. If you don't have a name I suggest the objective of your telephone call is simply to ask for the name of the contact and then put the phone down, knowing that you will call back a day or two later so that you can ask for them by name.

This is where using your contacts or business linking sites can help you. Once you have a name, the task becomes different and potentially easier.

A confident approach

So, invariably, the first thing you are going to need to do is handle the screening person. You should simply ask for the contact name and, in a confident fashion, ask to be put through. The usual response is a question?

- "Who is it calling?" quickly followed by

- "What company are you from?" and most likely

- "What is your call regarding?"

One approach that I have found works successfully is to act as though you know the individual concerned. Therefore, your opening is:

"Hello, this is Gary; could you put me through to Peter please?" You immediately sound as if you know Peter, even though you don't, and you will have a good chance of being connected.

You must have the answers ready for the follow-up questions, too, of course, so state your company and give your purpose as, "I want to talk to him about our meeting" for example.

Again, from the recipient's perspective, it sounds as though you have a meeting already planned. It is no more or less than a play on words, which will, on occasion, get you past the screener.

Create a great "hook"

It's true to say, of course, that it won't always work – there is no such thing as a foolproof method; it's about increasing your chances of success.

Now you have to be ready with what you want to say to the contact when you do get to speak with them.

If you start to stutter and hesitate at this stage, you are certainly not going to create a positive perception of yourself and what you have to offer if you don't sound confident, ready and prepared.

You need to have a "hook" statement prepared – something which is going to sound interesting enough to the recipient that they want to find out more. It is a good idea to offer a benefit that your product or service offers to companies in the same or similar industries.

The hook statement that you prepare needs to be customized and specific to the individual you are directing it to. Features and benefits will be covered in more detail in Chapter 6 - "Buildinging a winning proposition".

Give them benefits

My favored approach has always been: "We have many customers in similar markets to you who are enjoying great benefits from our products (or services)".

"I'd simply like to ask you a few questions about your business and processes so that I can decide which of our products will benefit you most. Would the 14th at 2:30pm suit you or would you prefer the 22nd at 10:30am?"

When giving an alternative, you are more likely to get a response stating which date preference they have. You may have to give a little more information than this, usually around what you are offering but I would suggest that you talk in general terms rather than be specific.

...cont'd

This gives you some flexibility to shape your proposition once you have, in fact, found out more about the prospect. As part of your preparation, be sure that you are ready to handle any objections that might be stated, even at this early stage.

Many people will have an image or perception of your company, brand or offering and feel that they already know enough to make a decision.

Anticipate what that could be and have some evidence ready to quickly dispel their misunderstanding about the benefits you can give.

Once you have handled any objections, you can go back to the date options previously given.

The key to this is confidence and preparation. Sound confident and even assertive with the screener and have your "hook statements" and objection handling evidence, ready to be delivered confidently and without hesitation.

Use your USPs

There is one exception to that rule (about talking generally rather than specifically) and that is simply when you have an absolute knockout USP (unique selling point).

What I mean here is that, if your company has invented the solve-all product for a specific industry or sector, then go right ahead and tell them that – how could they possibly refuse to see you?

Make yourself stand out

You have to remember that you are just one of a number of sales people approaching that prospect and attempting to sell their wares. Your goal must be to make enough of an impact to make the prospect agree to see you, as opposed to your competitors.

Also remember that your competitors, in the prospect's eyes, are not just those other companies who offer similar products or services to you butare also every single other sales person who is seeking to get time for a sales call.

One buyer will usually have responsibility for a number of products or product groups and they can't see every single person from every single company.

You are fighting for their valuable time and you will only get that by sparking some interest during your initial telephone contact.

When to call

One last thought – think about when to make that phone call. Is 9.00am on a Monday morning really the time when the recipient of your call is likely to be in the right mood to be open to your request for a meeting? I don't think so.

Equally, 4.45pm Friday will probably get the same response. But early on a Friday afternoon might catch someone in a receptive mood as they look forward to their weekend break.

I would suggest that you avoid before 10.00am on every day because that's when people are getting the day started, checking or sending e-mails and just generally waking up. Late morning/ early afternoon will often be a good time, both physically and psychologically.

The rule of thumb here is to apply common sense about your own situation. Think about when **YOU** would be most receptive to a call from an unknown source.

Although we are all different, the chances are that, if you consider it a good time, so will the other person.

Just be ready to handle the objections and have an alternative day and time prepared to agree for a call back.

Summary

- Understand your ratios. Each one of us has a set of ratios that work and determine the activity we need to get involved in to achieve the goals that we have set ourselves. Make sure you know exactly what those ratios are and then work them

- Use all available tools to create a "stock" of prospects who you can convert into loyal customers. By exploring existing databases, your existing contacts, and internet networking sites, you can easily have enough potential to work through

- Making contact through "warm" introductions will usually be much more productive than cold calling. Use existing contacts to introduce you; you will get a much more receptive welcome

- Be ready to get past the "gatekeeper". Have a technique that is tested and trusted and that you are, therefore, comfortable with. This will ensure that you don't use unproductive time attempting to get through to your chosen contact

- Create a strong "hook" to convince prospect contacts to see you. Once you have their ear, you need to be able to convince them that sharing their valuable time with you will be beneficial

- To increase your odds of success in gaining commitment to a meeting, make your telephone calls to prospects at a time of the day that is likely to be convenient for them. Calls first thing on Monday morning or late Friday afternoon are unlikely to be greeted with a warm reception

4 Building Relationships

Help people buy

Hot tip

People prefer to buy than be sold to. See your role as that of someone who is going to help the contact make a good buying decision, by presenting a compelling case for value and quality.

There is a fundamental belief I have, which is paramount in understanding why people buy what they do and from who they do. Whatever their needs and wants, most of us like to "buy" rather than be "sold to". Somehow, being "sold to" has the feeling of being forced or pressurized into a decision, which you didn't want to make.

You will probably be able to relate to this yourself if you think about your own experiences, when you have been looking to make a purchase. Do you like to walk into a store and immediately have the helpful sales adviser spring onto you like a leech and try to sell you something; anything?

Or do you prefer to look around and then ask for assistance as and when you feel you need some more information about the product or service you are interested in? I suspect most people reading this will say the latter.

Start asking questions

The customers, or prospective customers, who you go to see will be just the same. So your job is to help them make a good buying decision rather than try to sell to them.

I'll talk about questioning techniques later in the book, as only by asking the right questions will you find out what your customer wants and needs and then be able to help him or her make that good buying decision.

Some call this Needs Satisfaction Selling and that makes perfect sense to me –

1 Find out what your prospect needs

2 Then do all you can to satisfy it

This approach will undoubtedly improve your chances of success because, by giving your prospect customers what they need, you therefore make their buying decisions much easier to make.

Don't make assumptions

Do remember, of course, that we all do things our own way, so, just because we know how WE like to buy, it doesn't mean that you have found the secret to sales success. We are all different.

But by being aware of those differences, you can discover the style and approach that will make you a member of the "Successful Sales Club" – rather than the "also rans" who make up about 80% of the sales population.

There is a Golden rule that many people hold to be a true and a fundamental rule of life. In fact, our parents probably told us this as we grew up and, therefore, it tends to be at the core of our behavior and values.

"Treat others how we would wish to be treated ourselves".

Give them what they want

It is my belief that it is an entirely inaccurate rule to follow. The true Golden rule is "to treat people how they would like to be treated".

You may think me pedantic, however, the minor difference in words makes a complete difference to your behavior. Finding out how people want to be treated is the key difference we need to identify and act upon.

There are many studies and publications relating to different character types, how to recognize them and how to deal with them in the most effective way. Investing some time in reading these subjects will pay valuable dividends during your relationship building and proposition delivery.

Different personalities

One particular study I would recommend you read is by Dr. Susan Dellinger and describes people's characteristics in the form of shapes.

She has developed four main profiles, which cover most character types, and a fifth, which is effectively "all of the above" – in other words, those people who are unpredictable and will change their own behaviors and responses at various times you meet them.

...cont'd

Those are the most difficult to handle well, as you simply don't know what you will be faced with each time you meet or talk to them.

The good news is that most of us are fairly consistent in our behaviors and, therefore, we can be characterized and handled appropriately.

Each shape Dr. Dellinger describes has a list of typical behaviors, which enables you to understand what type of people they are. She describes:

1 the language they are likely to use, and

2 the issues that are likely to be important to them.

She then used those elements to describe the most effective approach in dealing with those people and, conversely (but just as importantly), what styles are likely to be least effective in building relationships and creating strong relationships.

I like Dr. Dellinger's model because it is simple to understand and enables you to easily characterize those people you interact with.

She then gives you all the answers in terms of how you need to behave to ensure you interact in the most effective way.

Perceptions

Create positive perceptions

The perceptions of you made by prospects and customers alike will be critically important, particularly in the early stages of your relationship building.

Any prospect company will want to have very positive perceptions of the individuals and companies they do business with. They want to be able to trust and believe in:

1 You

2 Your products

3 Your approach to your trading relationship

Those perceptions will be formed and influenced by your behavior from that first point of contact and throughout the relationship you have as you continue to trade with each other.

Although your company and its products are fundamental in the buying decision that is ultimately made, as an individual, you have a huge influence on the perceptions developed and you need to be constantly aware of what affect your behavior is having from the customer's perspective.

In general terms, you can categorize people as either

- Positive

or

- Negative

The chances are that the positive people are high achievers and, conversely, the negative are low achievers. That generalization is not true of every situation, of course, however, it's a pretty good rule of thumb.

Which do you want to be?

How would your friends and colleagues classify you?

Beware

Be careful of creating negative perceptions of you or your company through misplaced actions or words, especially early on in the relationship building. Once created, negative perceptions can be difficult to change.

Hot tip

If you can recognize your customer's personality type and preferred communication style, you can adapt your own methods to form effective, productive and beneficial relationships.

...cont'd

Get some feedback

Why not ask them and, when they give you their answers, ask them the reasons why – we rarely see ourselves as others do, so maybe this is your chance to get some good quality feedback, which you can use to maximize your own achievements.

But be ready – you may hear something that surprises or even shocks you! You need to know how you are perceived because, if your friends see you as a negative person, the likelihood is that your customers will see you that way, too.

Naturally, if they view you as a positive person with a good attitude, you can build on that perception in a very productive way.

Making life easy for others

One of the significant issues you need to consider is how you can make life as easy as possible for other people.

1   Take time to review the customer contacts

2   Attempt to understand what issues make life difficult for them, either from their individual perspective or their organizational perspective

Most of us would relish a trading relationship that was easy to manage, delivered those critical elements that we need and was an enjoyable experience in whatever contact we had with the other organization. Don't assume that it's all about product or service; it rarely is. Think about what things you can do to ensure all runs smoothly and, when it doesn't, react quickly and positively to resolve whatever issue has arisen to cause disruption.

The dynamics of customer contact

A simple element to your working relationships with your customers will be contact; how, who, when, and what frequency. In your early contact with a prospect, you have the perfect opportunity to get this right and establish the communication pattern that suits the other person. Simply ask what they would like:

● How often do they want to see you?

● When is most convenient?

● What information would they prefer in written form? (letter or e-mail)

● Who else do they want you to communicate with?

This is about as fundamental as it gets, however, many sales people don't ask the questions and, therefore, don't get it right. So set yourself apart from the crowd by giving your customer contact what they want, when they want it.

Don't forget

By building broad contact surfaces through the inclusion of other relevant people from both organizations, the relationships becomes much stronger, longer lasting, and more difficult for your competition to break.

Creating a strong bond

Making the relationship strong

Apart from the relationship you will build individually with your customer contact, your ability to include other people in the trading relationship between your two companies will largely dictate:

- Just how strong that relationship is, and

- How well it will withstand not just competitive threats but also any other hiccups you experience along the way, such as stock or quality situations

I have worked with many sales people who have held on to customers their current proposition and value did not give them a right to hold.

The reason they were successful in maintaining that trading relationship was that they had worked hard on building solid relationships between the organization they represented and the customers organization. Let me explain in graphic terms why this aspect of relationship building is so important:

If you attempt to join two triangles together at the point, the bond will be weak:

If, however, you join two triangles together at the base, the bond will be strong:

The key, therefore, is to have as many relevant points of contact as possible to secure the "join".

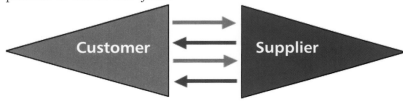

For example:

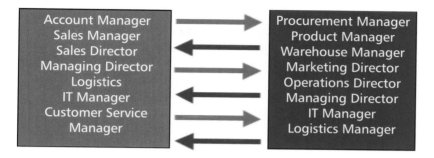

Account Manager Sales Manager Sales Director Managing Director Logistics IT Manager Customer Service Manager	Procurement Manager Product Manager Warehouse Manager Marketing Director Operations Director Managing Director IT Manager Logistics Manager

As well as creating that "bond" between the organizations, it also demonstrates a Partnership relationship between the supplier and the customer.

People buy from people
People really do buy from people.

Of course, you need the right product or service, however, it's also true to say that many good sales people hang onto business their proposition alone gives them no right to have.

The reason is simple:

- they have built a sufficiently trusting relationship with their customer that they are given leeway when it comes to product or service performance or value

This really can't be underestimated and it should always be your goal:

- to build such good relationships with your customers that they will find moving to a competitor extremely difficult

The opposite is, therefore, true:

- Nobody will buy from you if they don't like you very much

It's just the same as any other relationship – the more you like each other, the more time you will want to spend with each other.

Don't forget

People buy from people. If the contact likes you, they are more likely to buy from you – the reverse is also true.

57

Building trust

The importance of trust

Nobody will buy your product if they don't trust you.

If an unprofessional looking door-to-door salesman arrived on your doorstep, would you buy from him? It's the same, whatever product you are selling to whatever customer – that customer must be able to trust you as well as the company you represent.

Then they are much more likely to trust your product or proposition. Don't attempt to skip this part of the sales process, because, in many ways, it is perhaps the most important part.

There are so many ways to build trust, of course, and not being a pushy sales person is one of them. Think about what makes you trust someone:

1. Do what you say you will do

2. Demonstrate that you are honest

3. Be discreet about sensitive information

4. Clearly show you have integrity

5. Don't gossip about other people

6. Don't condemn competitors

7. Be a nice person to deal with

Nothing will turn your customer against you quicker than you demonstrating that you cannot be trusted to keep sensitive or confidential information to yourself.

Building confidence

Give others confidence in you

Trust develops when people feel totally confident that the other person or company won't let them down.

The integrity of the product, service and relationship is without question and there is a great feeling of mutual reward and success from the trading relationship you have.

This does, of course, take time to develop, but it is also true to say that it can be developed quite quickly if you do the right things at the right times.

As I said before, doing what you say you are going to do is a great place to start. That's something you can do on your very first meeting and it's a good idea to create that situation so you can demonstrate your ability to operate with complete integrity and trust to your prospect.

1. Fulfill your commitments

2. Demonstrate your knowledge and expertise

3. Show excellent understanding of customer needs

4. Be efficient, if you demonstrate your product

5. Show sensitivity to those around you

6. Deliver an outstanding all-round package

Making an impression

Creating the right impression

Remember that you are making an impression and creating an image as soon as you pull up outside the company premises.

Anyone looking out of their window when you park your car will make some sort of judgement immediately. It might be about the type of car you are driving (which, assuming you are employed, you are unlikely to have much control over) and it will certainly be about the condition of your car.

Make sure you are ready to greet your audience before you leave your car – don't walk up to the reception while adjusting your tie or straightening your shirt collar. It's simply not professional.

An advantage that you can use is that there does seem to be a real 'dressing down' among sales people in recent years, so your ability to seem totally professional in comparison is increased.

1 Look professional

2 Walk properly

3 Talk politely

You have already started to build that relationship.

4 Finally, don't forget to smile.

Looking the part

Dress for the occasion

The relaxation I mentioned in the last paragraph means that the expectation about the way you dress is different from how it was some years ago.

In the sixties, it was deemed normal practice for sales men to wear white shirts (never grey or blue) and often a trilby hat. So dress appropriately for your audience.

Dressing down is much more common now but do beware – don't dress down TOO much. The days of dark suits, white shirts and dark ties may well be disappearing… BUT that doesn't mean you shouldn't be smart.

Dressing according to the environment your customer sets is probably acceptable, but I would still urge you to be more formal with a suit and tie. And if you wear a tie, please do have your top button done up and tie pulled snugly up against your collar. It has become increasingly popular for men to wear the top button undone and it just looks untidy.

Be smart, not casual

Increasingly, this dress code will be smart casual, especially in high tech or media organizations. But remember, the first part of that description is SMART. Clean and pressed chinos and a shirt can still look very business-like, as long as they are clean and smart – and don't forget to polish your shoes.

Many people believe that you can tell a lot about someone by just checking whether or not they polish their shoes. It's about attitude and, if you can't be bothered to polish your shoes regularly, then maybe your attitude isn't what your company or customer is looking for.

I am amazed at the number of people who buy shoes and then wear them until the holes appear, having never seen a tin of polish. That relatively small detail can ultimately spoil your outfit and overall image.

Beware

Don't dress down too much just because your customer does. They still expect professionalism from you and it is far better to be overdressed than underdressed.

Don't be too familiar

Avoid being over-familiar

Once you get to know your customer well, there is a temptation to become over familiar or even flippant. Resist this trap because, however well you get on, your customer won't want to be taken for granted – and that's how it will seem.

Don't forget, this is about long-term strong relationships; your spouse or partner wouldn't expect to be taken for granted and nor should your customer.

Regular confirmation of the strength of your offering and the benefits you are delivering will ensure that you are not being taken for granted as a supplier either. The strongest relationships are mutually rewarding and satisfying. Keep them fresh and enjoyable – and long.

Know your audience

To a large extent, you have to make a judgement here because different people will find differing levels of familiarity acceptable and even preferable.

This is where your skills come in, understanding enough about the person you are dealing with to know where to pitch your level of familiarity.

This can become tricky when you have several important contacts within the same company. Don't allow yourself to behave inappropriately with one customer contact because of the relationship you have with another within that same organization.

Customer entertainment

Customer entertainment can be a very tricky situation these days. Many companies disapprove of their employees being entertained and, if this is company policy, you need to respect that. If, however, your customer is allowed to be entertained, find something different to do with or for them.

Naturally enough, it's great to take them to an event that is a favored hobby or pastime, but maybe that's what everyone else does. Try to find something that is memorable in its uniqueness and its excitement. You can be sure who that customer will remember most… and if you are creative, it doesn't have to take up your entire entertainment budget in one go.

Be different

Some of the other entertainment opportunities you could use are the theatre and concerts, industry events or experiences such as driving at a circuit, hot air ballooning and spa treatments. The key is simply to give your customer something that is special for that particular person.

Getting to know you time

Entertaining your customer doesn't just give you the opportunity to ensure you and your company will be remembered. It also gives you a large time window to get to know him or her and to find out what really makes them tick – what their key motivators or critical issues are. Wherever possible, arrange to collect your customer and travel to the venue together. Depending on what you are doing, of course, you may get several hours in the car or on the train one on one to discuss all manner of things. You can yield more information on just one entertainment trip than in several sales calls.

The atmosphere is also conducive to having a more open conversation and you will often glean information that you would never be told in the work environment. But be careful – don't assume that the friendly environment you are in allows you to ask impertinent questions – they may cause offence. Of course, your customer has come for an enjoyable and enriching day out, so don't use it as too much of an interrogation session, however tempting that scenario might be. You are there to cement relationships, to thank your customer for their business and to look forward to a mutually rewarding trading relationship in the future.

Customer relationship security

Keeping things secure

Having achieved a solid and trusting business relationship by going through the stages outlined in this chapter, how do you then go on to protect it?

The answer to that question is one that has many elements to it:

1 Continue doing the things you have done so far to get to this stage

2 Ensure that you make the number of people within each company (yours and the customer's) who have contact with each other as large as possible. (Refer to Chapter 13 on Key Account Management, which goes into more detail). Every single one of those people acts like a finger on the hands of the relationship, interlocking with each other to create the strength that you need. The more fingers that interlock, the stronger the bond

Internal relationships

Use your colleagues productively
The whole business-to-business relationship tends to be thought of as one company having a connection with another; and, of course, that's true.

For the sales team, those relationships should go two ways:

1 Externally to the customer and the key contacts within that organization

2 Internally to every department or function that can influence the offer being given to that customer

It's very easy for us to ignore that point and there will come a time when you will wish that you had better relationships with your colleagues; especially when a crisis develops and you need help to resolve it.

1 Get them involved with your customer

2 Take them in on field visits, and

3 Take time to make them feel involved

The list of people you should consider building strong relationships with will inevitably vary from company to company, depending on its structure and make up.

Consider the following list – maybe you have these roles within your own organization and could include them:

- Sales administration
- Marketing
- Customer service
- Research and development
- Technical service

- Logistics
- Stock control
- Credit control
- Training
- I.T.

Summary

- Most people prefer to "buy" than to be "sold" to. Adopt an approach that enables your customer to buy easily and with confidence

- Treat people how they want to be treated, not as you "think" they wish to be treated. You will stand out from the crowd if you do that which immediately gives you a USP

- Most people will acknowledge that perceptions are more important than reality. Therefore, you must ensure that you are aware of the perceptions you are creating, and, of course, that they are positive

- For your relationship to be strong and loyal, you need to create a network of contacts from each organization talking to each other. Apart from other benefits, it means that if one person leaves one of the organizations doing business together, the bond will remain strong

- Much of your relationship with your customer will be built on trust. It is critical that you are constantly aware of your behavior and actions and how they might impact on the trusting partnership that you need to create and maintain

- Create the right impression at all times, whether it's the way you dress, what you say or how you behave. Even when you have formed a good relationship, beware of being over-familiar

- Despite many restrictions that many companies place on corporate entertainment, spending time with your key customer contacts can prove invaluable in both creating and then maintaining that essentially strong trading relationship. Wherever possible, travel with your contact so that you get extra "one-to-one" time with them

- Never underestimate the power and value of your internal relationships, too. Colleagues can and will help you maintain a great value proposition through their own efforts, regardless of their function or role

5 Information Gathering

Don't sell too early

I have lost count of the number of times I have been working with a sales person and, as soon as we get into the sales call, they start to deliver their pitch.

They get the niceties out of the way and then start firing benefit bullets at the customer or prospect. Now take into account that so far they know very little about:

● Who they are talking to

● What that person or company's critical issues and drivers are.

Despite not being aware of this information they go straight in with all of the reasons why they should take an order right here, right now.

So far, in my sales career I have never seen this approach work successfully in creating a new long-term customer. You must start the sales cycle by asking good quality, directional and consultative questions about:

● The Company

● The contact's needs and wants

● Opportunities for you to show a competitive advantage

Only then can you hope to convert this Prospect into the life-long customer you are striving for.

Blueprint your customer

I call this part of the sales call 'blueprinting' because you are effectively drawing a blueprint of your customer, in order for your own personal decision-making to be of a greater effectiveness, in terms of shaping your proposition to maximise your chances of conversion (remember your ratios?).

Where is the information?

One of the key objectives of your customer meeting is to gather information, of course. However, don't assume that you have to wait until that meeting starts before you start to get useful intelligence that will help you later in the process. Take a good look around while you are waiting to see someone; there may be clues around the reception area or showroom that will give you a steer on how to position your opening statement. Look for their own Mission Statement, which will contain not just their goals and objectives but also their company "values" – both of which will enable you to develop your "hook" statement, which you need to deliver to gain immediate interest in both you and your products or services.

You may be able to establish information like:

1. Who are their other suppliers?

2. What do they make/sell?

3. What is their Decision Making Unit (DMU) – who makes the decisions?

4. What is the Decision Making Process (DMP) – how do they go about it?

5. Does it give the impression of being an innovative company?

6. Is quality likely to be a key factor for them?

7. Are there award plaques or certificates hanging proudly on the walls?

...cont'd

Hot tip

Use your traveling time to remind yourself of your objectives for your next meeting. Rather than putting on your radio, just think through what you want to achieve and how you will handle potential objections.

There are always clues if you look hard enough and you can interpret what you see; so keep looking and make some notes to ensure that you don't forget.

This is an opportunity to make good use of the time you are going to be losing as you wait for your meeting to begin, so use it productively.

Invariably, company reception areas will have trade publications that can give invaluable information on critical sector issues, which, apart from increasing your overall industry knowledge, might give you interesting topics of conversation in the early stage of relationship building.

You may also discover articles or advertisements for other companies in that sector who could become additional prospects for your products, too.

Knock yourself out!

And don't forget to have that knock-out opening statement ready to deliver very early on after you have introduced yourself.

This needs to be something that will catch someone's attention instantly and make them want to find out more.

I can't tell you exactly what that should be because I don't know your product –

- use a Unique Selling Point (USP) if you have one, and, if you don't, then

- use a Key Selling Point (KSP).

This enables you to make an immediate impact.

Sources of information

Good information sources

Talk to anyone and everyone that you can.

Receptionists, in particular, are a great source of information, and what surprises me most is that the majority of the people those receptionists 'process' in any given day don't speak to them other than to give their name, company and point of contact.

If you strike up a conversation with them, you are likely to get some valuable information you can use, either then or at a later date.

Furthermore, they will remember you the next time you call, which can only be a positive thing.

Ask some general questions about the company, its business sectors and customers. Try to find out if any of your competitors supply them or if they know other sales people from related suppliers whom you may know yourself.

They then become useful sources of information for you to make contact with at a later date. Just one word of advice: receptionists are often also responsible for fielding the phone calls the company receives, too, so be sensitive to that and don't try to keep them talking when the call lights are flashing.

Say that you will wait while they answer that call and then resume your conversation once they have finished. This should be obvious and simply good manners; however, I have seen many sales people be oblivious to simple sensitivities, which can make or break the willingness of that individual to become a good source of information for you.

The same is true of security staff – they know everyone who goes in and out of that building so might be able to give you some useful information, if they are approached in the right way.

The simple rule is to be friendly and not interrogate them. If you ask your questions in a conversational style, you are likely to get a good response and some useful information to help you in your quest to make this a new customer.

Customer meetings

Once you get in front of a customer, it is critical that you make the meeting as productive and beneficial as possible to both parties.

You are both investing your very valuable time and you are in a position to now start creating very positive (or negative…) perceptions of yourself and your organization.

To ensure that happens, it's worth asking the prospect at the point you make the appointment - your telephone call - if it would be beneficial to have any of their colleagues at your meeting. Just by asking that question, you are demonstrating to the contact that you want to ensure that the time spent together is productive.

You must plan thoroughly for each meeting, rather than turning up with an attitude of "seeing how it goes". That planning should include considering each party's:

- Positions

- Needs

- Critical issues

Set yourself objectives

Make sure you have considered your own objectives for the meeting; what do you want to specifically achieve before the meeting closes? You should have:

"Primary" objectives. This may be getting commitment from the customer to progress trials of your product or services.

"Secondary" objectives. This might simply be information gathering and to start the critical action of relationship building.

It is absolutely true to say that "people buy from people" and, as soon as you have that first telephone call, you are beginning to build a relationship and create images and perceptions you will obviously want to be positive.

Customer's objectives

Now consider what the other party would like to get from the meeting – also ensure that you ask that at the start of the meeting.

It will demonstrate to the prospect that you care about his or her time and company as well as giving you warning of what you need to provide as part of the time spent together.

You can pre-plan this element, too:

● you will know the role or function of who you are seeing so, based on your experience, you can anticipate those issues that are likely to be critical and important to them

● Be careful not to make assumptions at this stage – you are simply planning what topics to cover and how you will position your own company to address those anticipated critical issues

● It's important that you ask good quality questions at the meeting, to enable you to shape your proposition into a winning one

Anticipate objections

At some point during this first meeting, you may encounter objections to proceeding, and you must be ready for those.

If you receive those objections and cannot immediately respond positively and without hesitation, you are in danger of the meeting ending prematurely and, therefore, before you have managed to gather all the information you need and want to obtain.

This is where, once again, you can use your previous experience in this or other sectors.

● What objections have you received before?

● What statements can you make in response, which will justify your position or proposal and allow the conversation to progress towards the objectives you had previously set for yourself?

Too many times, sales people do not plan this element of the meeting and, consequently, when faced with a significant and very real objection from the customer, fall short with their response.

...cont'd

You need to be:

- confident

- articulate

- clear in how you handle that situation

Customers will interpret hesitancy or apparent lack of confidence very negatively and are unlikely to want to continue the conversation.

How much time?

Finally, ensure that you establish how much time you have. Even if you have agreed this during the telephone call that set up the appointment, it is still a good idea to confirm that alongside the agenda at the start of your meeting.

Once you have confirmed how long you have, it's your responsibility to keep a subtle check on the time to ensure that you finish on time and with all objectives from both sides met.

Because this is the early stage of relationship building, you have an immediate opportunity to impress your customer contact. Like you, your contact will have pressures on their time as well as their own "time stealers". By being in control of the meeting and ensuring that all objectives are met, you will encourage them to meet you again – they will have a perception of you as being efficient and effective as well as professional and considerate.

Those "hooks" again

I talked earlier about "hook" statements that will immediately gain attention and interest. Like the other elements of planning, you should have these well prepared and tailored for the specific industry sector and function of the person or people you are seeing. You want them eager to find out more about you and your proposition and, therefore, enthusiastic about sharing information that will help you formulate that winning proposition later in the sales process. The question you need an answer prepared for is simply:

- "Why should that customer change suppliers to you?"

- If you can't answer that question confidently and persuasively, how do you expect them to make the change?

Ask LOTS of questions

Prepare your questions

The method that I have always used for questioning (and would encourage others to adopt) is:

- draw up a form for completion in front of the customer that details all of the important information you will need

I would suggest that you decide on typical information that would be both useful and worthwhile for you to collect, and then create a form to use in each prospect call based on your decisions. (This is very easy to create with a Word document on your PC.)

By using this method, you not only ensure that you don't forget to ask something, but you can also create your own database of customer information by transferring your notes, onto your PC later that day or week.

Silence is golden

So the solution is simple

- ask a question… and then shut up!

Even if there is silence for a while, don't feel obliged to fill the gap with whatever comes into your head first.

This is merely thinking time and you will get your answer, as long as you give the customer the opportunity to talk in their own words.

If the situation is rather difficult, perhaps in a negotiation situation, that silence from you is incredibly powerful so it is even more important that you don't break it.

Hot tip

Create a question template with your computer, which will enable you to get all the information you need without constantly thinking about your next question.

Get some feedback

How are you doing?

This is not as simple as it seems for some people.

They seem to feel compelled to offer their own answer so, if this is you, practise just asking questions and then being totally quiet while you wait for the response.

You may not realize that you do this so ask your family, friends and colleagues… not all of us are very self-aware and we tend to do things without even realizing that we are doing them.

This is really important, so take some time on it and practice, practice, practice!

Very few Sales Skills courses I have witnessed take enough time on covering questioning techniques and I believe that it's the foundation for all that follows.

When do I ask questions?

The simple answer to that question is 'at every opportunity'.

Questioning is not an activity that happens on the first or second sales call only. Every time you are in a contact situation with your customer or prospect, find some questions to ask.

If you know the customer very well, those questions might be very simple ones about the current activity within the organization or market.

There is always something that you don't know and it will prove very useful to you later to have the maximum amount of up-to-date knowledge possible about your customer and the market they operate in.

Stock questions
If you can't think of any specific questions to ask, you can fall back on some basic ones, like:

"How is the current economic climate affecting your market?"

"Which part of your manufacturing process is giving you the biggest headache right now?"

"Is there one thing that you would change within your manufacturing process if you could?"

"What things are causing you the greatest concerns at the moment?"

One of the questioning techniques you can use to ensure you get the information you need is the use of "directional questions".

...cont'd

These are simply questions on specific topics you want to understand better.

Examples are questions like:

> *"What issues are you faced with when......?"*
>
> *"How do you feel about............?*
>
> *"If ......happened, what effect would it have on your manufacturing process?"*

Naturally, you need to fill in the gaps to tailor those questions to the specific areas of interest for you and your product or service offering.

The answers to these questions will give you the opportunity to establish key issues and then probe further with follow-up questions, such as:

> *"How does that impact on you?"*
>
> *"What do you currently do to resolve that situation?"*
>
> *"What would prevent that from occurring in the first place?"*

This will help you to really understand the situation and, perhaps more importantly, the reasons behind the decisions that have already been made by that company at that time.

As before, this will enable you to shape your own proposition to then maximize the chances of success in bringing this company into your list of customers.

Needs satisfaction selling

Give them what they want

I mentioned Needs Satisfaction Selling earlier.

Just think, if you could help make just one of those situations better with your own product or service, how pleased would your customer be. That would then lead not just to more business right now, but also to increased credibility and trust fin the future.

Many a salesman has lost business because they stopped asking questions throughout the relationship and made incorrect assumptions about their customer's wants and needs.

The other "sin" is the lack of communication, which means that your customer is buying a competitive product or service simply because they didn't know that you had the product or service in your portfolio.

This always happens as a result of insufficient questioning and, therefore, an inability to truly and comprehensively understand your customer's needs.

"Open" questions

Hot tip

"Open" questions start with "who", "how", "what", "why", etc. and encourages dialogue rather than short, one word answers.

Information gathering questions

In the early stages of a business relationship in particular, it is a very good idea to ask "open" questions. These are questions that make the other person give you information rather than just answering yes or no.

So, for example, ask how they currently make their world famous widget?. Your customer will have to give you lots of useful information, which may help you later on in the sales call. Open questions will typically - but not always - start with 'how' or 'why'.

Clearly you need to ask different questions depending on what you are trying to find out or establish. For example, if you want to gather information, ask questions like:

"Why did you decide to do it that way?"

"Who have you had success with previously?"

"What prompted you to make this enquiry?"

"What do you need this product/service to do?"

"What is going to be the best way of making this happen?"

"What challenges does your current process create?"

"What are the best things about that process?"

"Closed" questions

Confirming information

Closed questions are those that, usually, only require one word answers, like "yes" and "no".

They are still very useful but will not open up further avenues of discussion in themselves. The best time to use closed questions is when you want to pin down something specific, and to qualify it. Examples of questions such as these are:

> *"Do you have any time restraints for making this happen?"*
>
> *"Is anyone else is involved in this decision?"*
>
> *"So, if I understand you correctly, the fact that your current supplier can't deliver on Fridays is a real problem to you?"*

What a great opportunity for you, especially if you can deliver on Fridays.

In that example, you could respond with a huge benefit by simply stating that you can and will deliver on Fridays and

> *"When would you like the first delivery to be made?"*

In its own way this type of question is just as powerful as an information-gathering question – it simply offers different information and should be used at different times.

Don't forget

Use "Closed" questions to pin down specific information you want to confirm. It's a good summarizing technique and demonstrates that you are listening.

Active listening skills

Show you are interested

Now that you have managed to get your contact to talk to you about the important business issues, it should be obvious that you must listen to the answers they are giving to you.

Most importantly, as well as listening, you should also demonstrate that you are listening by using 'active listening' techniques. These are simply actions on your part, that convey your interest and understanding of what is being said.

I think one of the reasons that many sales people don't listen as well as they should is because they are actually thinking about what they want to ask or what they should say next. While that is undoubtedly important, it's not useful if it means that your customer thinks that you are not listening to them.

Why should they bother to answer your questions if you are not going to listen to what they have to say?

Demonstrating good listening skills is actually relatively easy – using both verbal and non-verbal techniques.

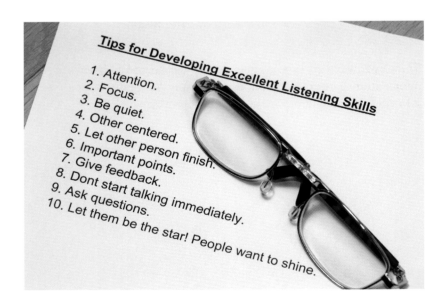

Tips for Developing Excellent Listening Skills
1. Attention.
2. Focus.
3. Be quiet.
4. Other centered.
5. Let other person finish.
6. Important points.
7. Give feedback.
8. Dont start talking immediately.
9. Ask questions.
10. Let them be the star! People want to shine.

Verbal

1 'Yes"

2 "I see"

3 "Uh-huh"

4 "OK"

5 "I understand"

6 "Let me just make sure I understand; are you saying that...............?" (summary)

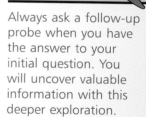

Hot tip

Always ask a follow-up probe when you have the answer to your initial question. You will uncover valuable information with this deeper exploration.

And so on.

Link your next question to the last answer you received.

Sound interested

In other words, encouraging words and sounds to ensure that the other person can be confident that you are not only listening to exactly what they are saying, but understanding it too.

The summary is your chance to paraphrase what has been said, to demonstrate that understanding.

Don't forget

The importance of your body language in all interactions with other people. Sometimes it's not what you say but how you say it that influences the other person's reaction.

...cont'd

Non-verbal

Look interested:

1. Good eye contact

2. Nodding your head

3. Lean forward a little

4. "Thinking" poses

5. Make notes

6. Being present – make sure you are concentrating on what is being said and not allowing your mind to drift elsewhere.

Great listening skills are vastly under-rated and should be developed as your default position.

Particularly when you are gathering information, your purpose is to listen much more than you talk. Ask those probing questions, sit back and actively listen to the answers.

Because you have two ears and one mouth, the rule of thumb is simple – listen twice as much as you speak. You'll be amazed at what you can learn and how you can use that newfound knowledge to great effect.

Get into the habit

Make it second nature

These good communication techniques come naturally to some people but not to many others.

Practice and planning is just as worthwhile with this skill as any other. Why go into "live" situations as your practice field when you can do so in a situation that holds no risks if you get it wrong?

Because we talk naturally and without too much thought, it would be easy to assume that we are all good communicators, however, your own experiences with others will demonstrate that the reality is quite different.

For you to stand out from the crowd, you need to ensure that you are as good as you can possibly be – which means

- practice

- practice

- practice

When you are talking to your friends and family, or indeed your colleagues, use the simple techniques I have described above until they become a habit.

I have mentioned the importance of forming good habits before and I really can't emphasise that enough. There is no doubt that those people, in whatever profession they have chosen, who have created good habits in what they do are invariably successful.

The other way of looking at it is that successful people almost always have excellent habits in the way they operate. Whichever way you view things, it's clear that forming those good habits will increase your odds of having a successful career.

Using role-plays

Practice makes perfect

Like many others, good communication is another skill, that is easily practiced, using role-plays at sales meetings for example.

Scripts can be written that can then be played out for maybe 30 minutes on a regular basis between colleagues, which will lead to good practice when you are in front of your customers.

Although many or even most people don't particularly enjoy role-playing sales situations, there is no doubt in my mind that they can be extremely helpful as a learning tool, to practise and perfect your own techniques for any given situation.

Whether it's for questioning techniques, customer meetings, handling objections or closing the sale, trying different techniques and styles in a safe, risk-free environment, where honest and objective feedback can be given, will help you hone your skills and, therefore, improve your performance and results.

Mental gymnastics

Stay on the right path

You will need a certain amount of mental agility when writing notes and asking questions at the same time.

I think it's a bit like driving a car – at first there seems to be too many things to think about and do, but you soon get the hang of it.

Don't worry about allowing pauses to occur as you finish writing what you have just been told. Your customer won't expect you to be able to write in shorthand, so will be happy to wait a few seconds as you finish taking the notes that will help you provide him or her with future benefits.

As well as being efficient for you, it also demonstrates that efficiency to your customer. As part of your trust building, you want your customer to know that you are someone:

- who is on top of things

- who is well-organized

- who is effective in remembering important issues and future activities

If you promise to do something after the sales call has finished, and your customer sees you write it down, there will immediately be an assumption that you will do it.

If you don't write it down, the reverse could be true.

Body language

More important than you think

I am not an expert on body language, more an interested bystander. What I do know is that it's probably more important in your role as a sales professional than you might realize.

There have been numerous books published about body language and communication and I've referred to one on Page 51 (Chapter 4), which I think you might find useful.

There are some really useful tips for you to bring into your day-to-day communications and I strongly suggest you invest your time in reading something that could bring you significant rewards and success.

Audio-books are such a good way to learn because, by the very nature of what we do, we spend a disproportionate amount of time in our cars traveling our territories from customer to customer.

I do think this is good thinking time for considering the next sales call, but maybe, at the beginning and end of each day, you could commit to listening to some learning as you travel to and from home.

Intonation

I have talked already about the importance of tone – now let's consider it in a little more detail.

Think about the people you enjoy watching or listening to and consider their tone. Are they mono-tone in their delivery? It's unlikely, because, otherwise, you probably wouldn't enjoy listening to them.

A varied tone, which is reflective of the words being used or the point being made, is far more interesting to listen to and take notice of.

This is particularly significant when you are being assertive. A strong but controlled and measured tone will ensure that your message is delivered clearly and confidently. A varied tone is comfortable to listen to, as long as it matches what you are saying.

This is an important issue during all of your communication but none more so than when you are delivering your business winning proposition. You need to be:

1. articulate

2. confident, and

3. clear about the detail of what you are offering.

Just listen to yourself

As before, try practicing by listening to your recorded voice and how it sounds when you vary your tone.

Find the right tone for you and your message, and practise delivering it until it's natural and confident. Remember, even though you might feel a little silly about making your tone change during a sentence, your audience won't think so.

Just analyze someone who you enjoy watching and listening to – maybe a colleague or a comedian or presenter on television. You will notice that they vary their tone to emphasize significant points or pieces of information, which makes them more entertaining and, therefore, interesting to watch.

Keep your eyes and ears open

Market intelligence

As the eyes and ears of your company, it is partly your responsibility to identify what the market needs, not only right now, but also to anticipate future demands and opportunities.

If you feed back those identified needs to your own organization, it gives you the opportunity to improve your offering over that of your competitors.

Many sales people under-estimate the impact and influence they can have in shaping the future proposition they will have the opportunity to present; and who better to have that influence than the people who have regular, first hand contact with the customers themselves?

It's true to say that many sales organizations will have a Marketing and Product Development Departments, which will engage in market research and customer/market profiling in order to understand the opportunities that exist and how best to exploit them.

That doesn't preclude you from having your own very significant input. In fact, your customers will frequently be more willing and enthusiastic about talking to you regarding future needs and anticipated industry changes, because it gives them a chance to talk about a subject that is very important to them, as well as influencing that future market and the way it operates.

This is also an area where your own business relationship will not only help the information gathering process but enhance the trust between you and your customer.

Asking about their anticipated future needs, and then delivering product against them, will ensure that your customer perceives you as a driver of change and your organization as one that delivers for it's customers.

Get yourself ready

Are you ready?

It might seem completely obvious that you should be thoroughly prepared mentally before going into your sales call. Although it should be a significant part of your preparation, it's remarkable how few people get themselves into the right frame of mind as they approach the customer.

I talked earlier about a positive attitude and it really is so important that you are able to get yourself into a very positive approach, ready for the challenge ahead.

For some, that's easy - they are naturally positive and enthusiastic people - but others are not, in which case, you have to prepare mentally to ensure you are "up" for the customer meeting you are about to have.

This will be particularly effective prior to a difficult sales call or negotiation. Emotion can play a surprisingly important part in our mental preparation and, therefore, performance, so it is a worthwhile activity to ensure you are able to be the best that you can be.

Summary

- Asking good quality questions will enable you to uncover the needs and wants of your contacts and their organizations. By doing so, you can match the value offered by your proposition with the buying needs of the prospect to form a mutually beneficial relationship

- Use all the people you come into contact with to gather valuable information. From Security to Reception and P.A., useful information can be gleaned to help you build a complete picture of the prospect company

- Customer meetings will be more effective if you have planned well in advance, setting yourself both primary and secondary objectives. You should also anticipate potential objections that you may receive, so that you can prepare suitable justifications to handle them promptly and effectively

- Use "open" questions to uncover information and "closed" questions to confirm information. Demonstrate excellent listening skills to ensure your contact feels that you are paying full attention to what they have said

- By following core principles of questioning and listening skills, you will soon develop good habits that will serve you well in gathering valuable information and building strong relationships

- Make sure that you understand the power of different communication elements and styles. Not only will your words impact your contact; the way you deliver them alongside your non-verbal communication will impact the perceptions that people make of you

6 Building a Winning Proposition

Adding value

Most customers will expect certain added value elements to your offering.

They are seen as a given because, as time goes, on we all want to increase our perceived value to our customers. That in itself will raise the bar as far as customer expectations are concerned. A great example is service delivery.

When I started in sales, it was quite reasonable for a customer to assume that an order placed today would be delivered in around two weeks' time. To improve the perceived quality of the service given to the market, most companies worked hard to knock a day or two off this delivery time.

Gradually, it has reduced and now, of course, so many suppliers offer, and customers expect, next day delivery. In some industries, the same day delivery is not only expected but demanded. That's almost the rule to entry rather than an added value aspect to your offering.

Change in expectations

That's how the Just in Time (JIT) approach to stock control was developed, where not only do you have to specify the day that you deliver but also the time that you will deliver.

So, to give unique perceived value to your customers, you have to find something that your competitors don't have the ability to give.

But be careful and keep watching; they might not give it now but you can be sure that they will very soon. Then you have to find something new yourself, as the bar will have been raised yet again.

Unique Selling Points (USPs)

Unique Selling Points (USP) are critically important in your creation of perceived competitive advantage and value when creating your proposition.

By now, you have uncovered as much information as possible from your customer and their needs and wants, now you have the opportunity to deliver against those established needs.

A USP is exactly what it says it is; something that you can offer that your competitors can't; something that makes your proposition stand out from the crowd as being something they just have to own or buy for their organization.

They will often be identified by Product Development and Marketing Groups within your organization (if you have them) but that's not always the case. One of the reasons marketing should identify them is that I would expect to see the USPs listed in any literature and packaging designed for product launches or introductions.

It is so important to recognize the value these USPs give you when delivering your proposition to your prospect or customer, so you must know what they are and how they will benefit that company or person you are propositioning to.

Translate the benefit

USPs need to be explained and understood to ensure that the connection can be made between the USP and the direct benefits that apply to the use of the product or service.

It is important that you present that connection to the person you are dealing with, rather than assume that it will be made. Also remember that benefits can be expressed in terms of benefits to:

- the organization
- the individual, or
- both

We might present products or services where perhaps the main benefit is time saving, which does benefit the company, of course, but also shows great benefit to the people within that company.

Knowing your Unique Selling Points is one of the most important

Hot tip

Ensure that you use your USPs – if you have them. By definition, they are impossible for your competitors to match.

Don't forget

Individuals will have needs and motivations that span both professional and personal objectives. Customizing the benefits you offer to those needs greatly increases your chances of success.

...cont'd

weapons in your armory and will make the convincing part of the sales process much easier.

Unique is best

Uniqueness means exactly that; there is no other like it.

The reality is, however, that the majority of sales people will not be fortunate enough to have a product with a true USP. So what then?

The answer is simple – you have to work with what you have got and use Key Selling Points (KSP) to create a statement about your product, service or company, which is sufficiently strong and compelling that it is unique in its entirety.

That uniqueness might be a combination of things you are able to bring together in a way that your competitors can't.

If you think about consumable products - maybe photocopying paper - assuming that the different weights of paper (gsm) are available from many sources, there doesn't seem to be much that's unique in that.

If, however, one company can bundle that with every other office consumable likely to be needed by any given customer, with an efficient on-line ordering system, electronic billing and Internet banking invoice settlement, that total package might be unique.

So there is your USP.

If you don't have anything unique

Key Selling Points

If you are in that unfortunate position of not having any USPs for your product or service, there is still hope for you. You need to find a way of minimizing the significance of other USPs in the market, or amongst your competitors, and concentrate on the benefits of your offering to using the Key Selling Points that you have.

Everyone has KSPs simply because they are the strongest elements of benefit your product or service delivers to the customer. Even though it isn't unique, it does still have benefits, even if the only benefit you have is the price.

It is both more rewarding and more satisfying to be able to sell on things other than price, but some organizations create their business plans and selling strategy around delivering the lowest market price. They lose the ability to positively affect both revenue and profit lines by selling USPs (which, by nature, tend to command higher selling prices), so they create a strategy that delivers other company benefits through lowest like-for-like market pricing.

Internet example

Take a lead

A hugely successful example of this would be Internet aggregator sites. These are the sites that you see advertised, at just one click of your mouse, to identify all of the best deals available to you online.

For example, they might be flights – you type in where you want to go and when, and, with that one click of the mouse, your screen is full of hundreds of companies offering you the latest deals on cheap flights to your chosen destination.

It's absolutely, and ruthlessly, price driven and those companies appearing at the top of your screen (it's actually called "top screen rate" in the industry) are most likely to get your attention and probably your business.

The volume that can be created by lowest market pricing can deliver cost savings elsewhere in your organization, which makes that strategy a winning one in terms of margin and profit.

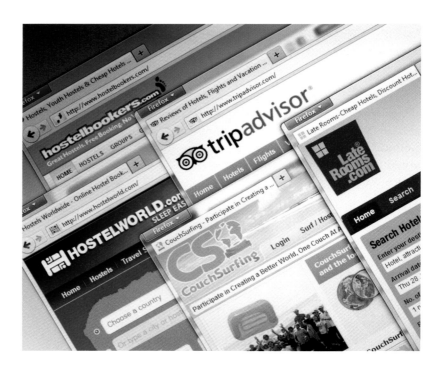

Show and tell

Show them what you've got

If you are selling a product, as opposed to a service, let your customer see your product... take some samples with you and put it or them on the customer's desk as you start talking.

Their natural curiosity will make it impossible for them not to pick it up and take a closer look. Being inquisitive is a characteristic of our human nature and you can use that to your advantage.

If you sell a service, take something they can look at instead; these might include photographs, glossy brochures or testimonials. As soon as they pick up the product or brochure, they are showing an interest (a potential buying signal) and you can start to talk positively about them owning and even using it.

It's almost time to go in for the order and, because your prospect has shown interest, it can be a gentle close.

Don't overwhelm them

As with most things in life, this is about balance – take enough samples to gain interest but not so many that you merely create confusion.

Invariably, if you have ten versions of the same thing but maybe in different colours, the customer will find one to choose. But because you have given so much choice, that decision becomes more difficult. If you offered four colors, the chances are that they would still find something that they like and would make the choice more simply.

How to use literature

Beware

Don't assume that the prospect who asks you to leave literature will ever contact you again – they won't! literature requests are simply a cowards way of saying "no thank you".

Do's and Don'ts of literature

Don't leave literature just because your prospect asks you to. That's the oldest brush-off in the book "Leave me some literature and I'll think about it". What he means is "I'm not interested but I haven't got the bravery or good manners to tell you to your face"!

If the customer wants to think about your proposition, tell them it's a good idea and why don't you think about it together?

Ask them what specific issues they will be thinking about. That way, you can help answer any questions that might be troubling them, or, at the very least, you'll find out why they don't want to buy your product or service right now. It's an objection and leaving literature won't handle it.

Literature can be a very powerful marketing and sales tool – but very few people buy anything from literature unless it's a shopping catalog for the individual consumer, which is a very different situation.

In commercial sales environments, people do not buy from the literature you have just left with them. They put it in their desk tray (if it makes it past the waste paper basket) where it's covered by the next piece of literature, left by the next sales representative to call.

The exception to the rule

My view is that the best time to leave literature is after you have taken an order and, therefore, started to do business together. By all means, leave them the information that will convince them that they have made a good buying decision.

It also gives them useful information about other products and services within your range, which might hold an interest for them, either now or in the future.

If they insist

I do accept, of course, that some prospect customers will insist that you leave them some literature and whatever you say won't change that.

I am not advocating that you refuse to do so – simply that you should do everything that you can to talk through any areas of uncertainty first, rather than rely on the person in question getting the information they need from your literature.

Don't fall into the trap of leaving literature in lieu of a more positive conversation.

Be an expert

Show your skill

Know your product. You may well have sales aids and literature, but you really have to know your product well in order to deliver a successful sales pitch.

When you are asked a question, you will create lots more trust in yourself as a sales person, as well as in your product, if you can answer straight away and with confidence.

Practise with colleagues or family to the point where you feel comfortable answering most questions regarding your product range.

Most organizations will give you product training periodically through your sales career – specifically at product launch time – which gives you a great grounding, but it shouldn't stop there.

Spend time going over the features and benefits of each product or product range to ensure that you can deliver them fluently and without hesitation when the opportunity arises.

Just imagine how you would feel if the person answering a question you'd put to them started to stutter and hesitate – how confident would you be?

Study for success

Over time, you will obviously become more competent at answering questions about your offering simply through experience.

In your early days, make sure that you practise and study to increase your knowledge and, therefore, your ability to be impressive. You can never know too much but you can definitely know too little.

Since a rather famous television advert some years ago, a new phrase has crept into the vocabulary of the average sales person: "I don't know but I know a man who does" or "I don't know but I'll find out and let you know". Now this isn't the worst thing you could say, and can be useful if you find yourself truly unable to answer a question, but it certainly doesn't instill confidence in your prospect or customer. So do everything you can to know as much as you can – not just about the features of your product or service but also the benefits it can bring to that customer.

Excellent demonstrations

Expert demonstrations

Practice demonstrating. If your product is one that can be demonstrated, make sure you are very good at doing so. Nothing will eliminate confidence in you and your product more than a poor or unsuccessful demonstration.

Conversely, an assured and impressive demonstration has a very good chance of sealing the deal. So make sure you practise over and over again before you attempt demonstrating it live – especially with a new product.

I liken this to a magician on stage. For that magician to be totally impressive, he or she needs to be slick, skillful and successful. If not, you won't believe the magic. The same applies to your demonstrations so make sure that you are slick, skillful and successful yourself.

Let them try it

Once you have carried out some form of demonstration, you should look for opportunities for the customer to try the product themselves.

This is particularly the case if you are selling a product used in a manufacturing process. Once you have shown the product in use yourself, give it to the person who will be using it in the future.

If that person likes what it does, they will be a great advocate for you and you are almost home and dry in getting that order.

Use your customer

I do accept that some people just do not have the aptitude for demonstration. They can practise over and over but they never seem to get it quite right.

In those circumstances, and only those circumstances, you should prepare the demonstration but give the customer operator the opportunity to try the product and, in effect, do the demonstration themselves. This really should be last resort though – don't use it as an excuse not to practise yourself to become the excellent demonstrator that will impress your customer.

Check your equipment and stock

Stock check

The preparation I spoke of earlier also applies to demonstration equipment and samples, too, of course.

You should set aside some time each week - maybe last thing Friday - to make sure that your demonstration equipment is in good working order, clean and presentable, and that any consumables you need are in good supply.

It is unforgivable to arrive at your prospect without the appropriate samples or equipment to carry out a successful demonstration. Remember that there is only one person who has control over that – you.

- The easiest way to do this is to keep an inventory of your demonstration equipment and any associated consumables

- Once you have created it to begin with, maintaining it will be easy and quick – simply edit your inventory each time you carry out a demonstration or leave samples, which means your records will always be accurate

- Then simply carry out your own stock check monthly to ensure accuracy, as well as giving you the opportunity to adjust stock levels according to forthcoming activity, new product launches, etc.

Stylish presentation skills

Influential presentations

The style of your presentation is going to strongly influence whether or not you will make a successful overall bid.

If you have thoroughly blueprinted (gathered good information) previously, you can tailor your content to match the needs and opportunities of your customer.

The more closely you mirror their situation, the more they will believe that you care about them and want to help them. We all like to be helped along the way at some point and this is a great start.

Don't forget to use a style that suits the individual you are talking to, i.e. a Managing Director and a shop floor worker will expect different things.

Being able to adapt your presentation to directly appeal to each of them is the key to being successful. Your ability to be a chameleon is directly linked to your likelihood of success.

Hot tip

Make sure you are slick and faultless when demonstrating products by practising at home or in your company premises, if the facility exists. Buyers like to be impressed by what they see.

...cont'd

Tailor your style

Again, preparation is key:

1 know your audience

2 Use this information to produce a proposition that will answer all the questions that might come to mind

3 Use this information for outlining the benefits and advantages that your product or service will give to them

Use appropriate vehicles of delivery, whether it's a PowerPoint presentation to a Board or a series of statements to a store floor operative.

Have your own style, by all means – if you can tailor that style to suit your audience, so much the better.

I mentioned Dr. Dellinger's research and findings in chapter 4 and there is nowhere better to use that model than in the presentation of your proposal.

This is when you are entering into the decision making stage of the whole sales process, so the more aligned your offering to the needs of both the organization and the individual is, the higher the likelihood is that they will accept your proposition.

Again, confidence is key in delivering a convincing and business winning proposition. Speak:

- confidently

- articulately

- with a level of friendliness or formality that suits the situation and your audience

Explain the benefits

Benefits not features

Always sell benefits – not features.

I'm afraid to say that the fact that your product is blue probably doesn't matter to the customer. What is important is what your product will do for that customer or their business. If you can tangibly show that you can:

- save money

- improve efficiency, or

- add value

how can you fail to take an order?

So by all means talk about the features, but it's the benefits that will make the customer want to buy from you.

Customize your benefits

Benefits can easily be developed in a generic form but that is not how you can deliver the maximum persuasion to your prospect customer.

I have mentioned "customized benefits" before and this is where we should explore them in more detail. During your information gathering stage of the sale, you found out the critical issues and needs of that organization and that individual or Decision making unit.

Now this is your opportunity to use that information productively in constructing a benefits package to satisfy the established needs and buying motives previously uncovered. This follows a simple formula, as shown in the diagram below.

Check that it benefits your customer

When you are preparing your customized benefit statement, you must ask yourself the question:

- "So what?"

If, after making your benefit statement, the customer can ask "so what?", it simply means that you have not defined the real benefit well enough.

Don't forget

Using "bundling" of benefits can often prove convincing, if single, small benefits are not proving compelling enough.

107

...cont'd

Hot tip

Write down the financial benefits your proposition offers, so your customer can see, in black and white, exactly why you should be their supplier of choice.

That's your rule of thumb and an easy way to challenge yourself after you have constructed your benefit statement.

If you can't ask that question, then there is a very good chance that you have created a real benefit rather than simply stating a feature of your product.

The other reason it's critical that you translate your product (service) feature into a benefit is that you cannot assume that your customer is able to make that translation themselves.

Invariably they can't; at least not as well and as convincingly as you can. Therefore, if you don't make that translation for them, you are in danger of losing the convincing benefit your product delivers.

The easy way to distinguish features from benefits is as follows:

1. A feature is a fact about your product or service – totally objective, such as size, color, and price.

2. A benefit is what that product will do for the customer – either objective or subjective, such as cost reduction, improve efficiency, reduced hassle, and reduced down-time.

When you make the translation from feature to benefit, you need a simple "connection" statement – something as easy as:

- "What that means to you is..."

- "The benefit to you is..."

- "Other companies with similar applications to you have found that..."

It couldn't be simpler.

The "Benefit Chain"

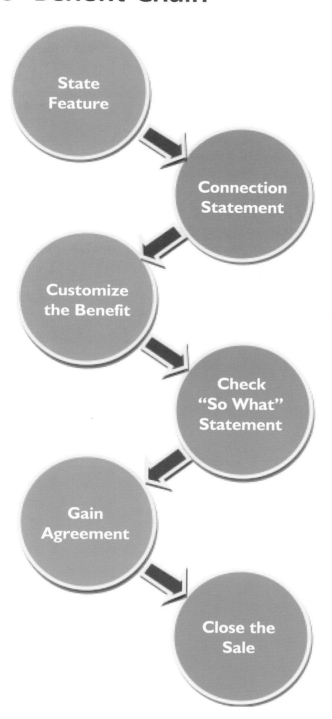

Pencil selling

Spell it out for them

You may have heard of a 'Pencil Sell', which is simply where you produce the information that supports your proposition on paper.

This can be incredibly powerful and it's worth the preparation before meeting your prospect. Always present the benefits of your product in the highest terms.

So talk about annual savings rather than unit savings, and annual profit gains rather than unit margins. Imagine yourself being presented with a proposition for a product that is 1p cheaper than the competition. It's not very impressive.

But if I told you that I use 4,000,000 units of that product each year and the saving would be £40,000 – it is a much more impressive value, so that's what you talk about.

Sales tools

Use testimonials

References and testimonials can be incredibly strong when trying to convince your customer to buy.

You can take (at least) two approaches to this issue.

1 Try to get testimonials from other companies that you know deal with your customer, so their opinion is credible and trusted. It may be a product that is used in conjunction with yours and, therefore, complements it well

2 You can also try using a testimonial from one of their competitors. If they think that their biggest rival has found a better supplier or method or cost, they will then be very keen not to be left behind. Play on that competitive nature and use it to your advantage

The power of testimonials from credible companies cannot be over-stated; here is a current user of your product or service who is strongly placed in the sector saying what a great benefit they have enjoyed as a result of buying from you.

When you say how good you are, the customer may not believe you simply because you are bound to say that and are, therefore, biased. When an independent and trusted company or person makes that same statement, your credibility immediately gets a massive boost.

Summary

- Make sure that you understand what "Added Value" your customer will want to enjoy. This differential will make you stand out from the crowd

- Not every company or product will be able to offer Unique Selling Points, but, if they do, make sure that you focus on them and the customer benefit they deliver to produce a knockout proposition

- Key Selling Points can be very effective and compelling, as long as you select those aspects that are going to deliver the best and most valuable customized benefits to your customer

- Practise demonstration of your products until you are an expert in delivery. This is your opportunity to show just how good your offering is and, therefore, why your prospect or customer should buy from you

- Make regular checks on your demonstration stock and equipment. If you turn up to demonstrate and find something isn't working, or stock is missing, you instantly create a negative perception, which will be difficult to eliminate

- Be wary of requests for literature if they are no more than an excuse to dismiss you. It's an old technique used by many buyers instead of being brave enough just to say "no" to you

- Tailor your presentation to the style and needs of your customer contact. The more you mirror your audience, the more you will increase your chances of success

- Ensure that you sell "benefits" not "features". People don't buy features of a product or service – they buy whatever those features will do for them. You cannot assume that the audience will have the ability to translate those features into realisable benefits and, therefore, you need to customize your presentation (whether it's formal or not) to focus on customized benefits for that contact and company

7 Tender Documents

Beware

Don't feel compelled to respond to all opportunities. If the outline doesn't look attractive to you, don't waste time and resources putting together a response document.

Tender process

In many industries and sectors, it has become increasingly common to award supplier contracts through the use of a tender process. This entails the issue of a request for information, which relates not only to the products or services in demand but also to other company information. This will then be used by the Decision Making Unit to make the contract award. These documents come in a variety of forms and names, the most common being:

- I.T.T. – Invitation to tender

- R.F.I – Request for information

- R.F.P. – Request for proposal

- R.F.Q. – Request for quotation

The core elements of these documents are intended to give more information about the capabilities of the potential suppliers to deliver an "all-round" service and a strong commercial package. Typically, they will include sections like:

- Executive Summary

- Timeline

- Deliverables

- Key personnel involved in the project/contract

- Evaluation criteria / weighting

- Payment terms

Although the commercial package is critical in this procurement process, it is not the sole piece of selection criteria. All elements will be taken into account, although each element may have a different weighting, which gives you a guide to where your strongest proposition needs to be.

More planning and preparation

As always, your planning and preparation is hugely important in your quest to win these sales opportunities. The first thing you

...cont'd

should be doing on receipt and acknowledgement of the tender document is to consider some of the key issues:

- Understand what information you should have gathered prior to compiling a bid document

- Outline what a compelling bid document should contain – from that specific customer's perspective

- Understand and outline how your document will differentiate your proposal from that of your competitors

- Understand how you can deliver on the buying criteria of the key decision makers – the DMU

- How to create the document using the right levels of text, information, graphics and in what layout, to ensure easy reading and compelling evidence

The first decision

Is it right for you?

The first thing you need to do is a relatively simple task – decide whether you actually want to bid for this work or contract.

It may seem obvious that all business opportunities should be explored and fought for, however, the reality is that, if you are not equipped well enough to deliver what the customer wants, you can do more harm than good by submitting your tender response.

You may be in a situation where:

- you do not have the capacity to deliver on expectations

- your competitive position might be weak in that product or service range

- strategically, the work or customer may not fit with your current direction

By submitting a sub-standard proposal, you will damage your image and brand with that customer and the key decision makers.

This might mean that, for future opportunities, you will be excluded from the tender process. Therefore, it is important that you, as an organization, consider:

1 your total package

2 competitive position

rather than automatically respond to the RFI because you feel that you should.

Preparation and planning

Key considerations

When starting your planning and preparation, there are some fundamentals you need to consider. This is not an exclusive list and you may have specific sector issues not covered here. If you prepare each relevant area well, you will increase your chances of a successful outcome:

- What is the decision making criteria AND its weighting?

- This will usually be stated in the original RFI

- What is the tender review process?

- What are the stages and will you be required to present your proposition after first filter?

- What is the required format/structure?

- Is it stated, and if not, how will you decide?

- Who will be part of the Decision Making Unit?

- Do you know the people concerned and how do they perceive your organization?

- What are the time-lines?

- Have you planned the resources and timing to ensure all deadlines are met without last minute rushes?

- What are the critical 'must have's' in the response?

- What are the critical issues? Without which you will fail in your bid

- What is our current relationship with the customer?

- Is it strong and could that strength help "weight" your proposition? (don't be complacent)

- What is the probability of your success?

- Based on previous experience, do you know whether you are likely to succeed in this RFI?

Hot tip

Delegate to make optimum use of each individual's skills and experience.

Hot tip

Make your document stand out from the crowd in its presentation. Yours will be one of many, and that immediate impact can influence the selection process.

...cont'd

- What are the needs and buying motives of the key decision makers?

- Have you established exactly what criteria you must deliver against for each member of the DMU?

- Who should be in the bid team and what are their individual roles and responsibilities?

- Have you made sure you have the right people; have you communicated what their responsibilities are and have you ensured that they have allocated sufficient time to deliver their role in this process?

- What is your exit strategy if you decide not to respond to the tender?

- How will you handle your refusal to issue a tender response while maintaining you relationship and credibility with the customer?

- What are the allowed communication channels during bid process?

- Many customers stop all communication during (or at specific stages of) the process. Have you established what your opportunities to communicate are?

- What are your key areas of strength?

- Have you established your Customized Benefits based on the buying needs of the individuals who you have identified make up the DMU?

- What are your key areas of weakness?

- Have you understood where you are weak to enable you to counter those weaknesses with your areas of strength?

- Where can you add "value"?

- Based on what the needs and desires of the customer are, have you identified those areas where you can add real value to make your proposition compelling?

- What time and resources do you need to compile the tender response?

- Have you ensured that you have the right people, with the right amount of time, to ensure a quality response within the given timescales?

Executive summary

The most important part...?

In some ways, this is the most important part of your tender response.

Of course, the commercial terms are critical and will often determine either the first filter or the final result. But it really isn't all about price, despite popular belief. Your overall:

- quality in product, service and delivery

- innovation

- customer support

- reaction time

- relationships and confidence

will all help with their decision making.

The Executive Summary appears at the beginning of the response document and sets the scene for what comes next.

It should be one page (two at the absolute most) and give a summary of what your offering will be and what it will deliver, in terms of customized benefits. It should be:

- a tempting read, which makes the decision maker want to turn the pages to reveal more of your proposition

- succinct and interesting, and

- it should be about your customer more than it is about your organization.

As a simple guide, the use of words about your customer (you, your Name) should be approximately 2:1 against those about your organization (we, our, us, Name).

It is, of course, true to say that your tender response is about your company and its proposition; the point is that the proposition should be about how you are going to satisfy the established needs of your customer. Tell them, in the Executive Summary, the highlights of those needs satisfaction. Make it easy for them to see why you stand out from the crowd and how you are clearly differentiated from your competitors.

Write it first

One more thing on Executive Summaries; they tend to be written at the end of the process, when the full response is complete and almost ready to go. They should be written at the start of your response composition. The reason is simple – as previously stated, this part of the response is the roadmap of the content of your offering and needs to be established at the start. By all means, edit it at the end, but it should be just that, an edit.

Checking the document

A fresh pair of eyes

Before your response is sent to your customer, it is critical that it is checked and critiqued by someone within your organization who:

1. understands the contract

2. understands the commercial offering

3. but has not been involved in the composition of that document

You need some objective and intelligent eyes with no prior involvement to read through and can, therefore, ensure that it is not only "fit for purpose" but compelling and persuasive.

To ensure that happens efficiently, alert a suitable candidate and ensure suitable time is allocated towards the due date, but with sufficient time so that edits can be made where necessary without it becoming a last minute race to the deadline.

Don't forget

Get an objective critique of your final document before it's submitted. Ensure that enough time is allowed for a final edit, if necessary.

Summary

- Although the structure of the document is often prescribed by the customer, the content within that structure is up to you. This is your opportunity to tell your compelling story, with customized benefits matching the identified customer neds and wants

- Don't feel compelled to submit a tender response every time you get an opportunity to do so. Think carefully about your ability to compose a winning bid – if you can't and end up producing an inferior proposition, you can do more harm than good by pitching for work you are not well placed to deliver

- As with so many elements of the Sales process, planning and preparation ais critical. Make sure you have a full understanding of your customer's needs and wants and, therefore, how you can position yourself as the supplier of choice

- The Executive Summary is arguably the most important element of the whole bid response. It should outline the key elements of your proposition as well as being the roadmap for your strategy to win this business. Some customer contacts will only read the Executive Summary and the Commercials and base their initial filtering decision on those elements. Therefore, it needs to be compelling, with strong customized benefits

8 Closing the Deal

Closing techniques

Beware

If you start closing before the contact is ready to buy, you will come across as pushy and that is likely to alienate and reduce your future chances of success.

Just ask for the order

As crazy as it may seem, the part of the sales call that many sales people seem to dread the most is asking for the order.

That's what you are there for, after all, but it can be a nervy situation – especially for someone new to sales. I think the reason this part is so difficult for some people is simply because of the fear that the buyer will say no – a rejection.

If that's the case, you just need to check why (Handling objections in Chapter 9 (Page 131) and do a little more restating of your benefits.

"Closing" is simply asking a question

There are many different ways of closing and most of them are not at all frightening.

This is simply another part of the sales process that both parties know will happen at some point and, therefore, shouldn't be avoided or worried about.

If you think back to the section about the idea of salesmen having the gift of the gab, it usually creates a perception of a high pressure closer who puts a huge amount of effort into making the customer buy.

It really doesn't have to be like that and you can take a very gentle approach. Before you know where you are, you will be tying up the loose ends of this first order.

Remember that "no" is simply a response to a question – just the same as "yes". So look for the buying signals - a statement, question or gesture that demonstrates interest in what you are offering - and ask if you can proceed with the order.

This is almost always perceived as the most difficult part of the sales call – but it really doesn't have to be.

Gentle "Close"

If, during your presentation or pitch, the prospect leans forward, it's a real sign of interest in what you are saying – so they might be ready to buy. This is a good time to ask a question as part of a 'soft' close:

> *"Do you feel that (what I have just described) would benefit your organization?"*

I'm quite sure that you don't need me to tell you that, if the answer is yes, you are certainly on the right path to a sale. So why not go for the full close and ask:

> *"Shall I arrange that for you?"*

It's not an aggressive close – you are merely asking your customer if he/she is ready to commit. It they are not, then you can continue with your presentation – nothing has been lost.

Of course, if they say yes, you have brought your presentation to an end earlier than you may have planned, which then gives you a little more time in the day to get one more sales call in.

Don't forget

Be brave! They can only say "no" and, if you have explained the benefits correctly, they probably won't.

125

Ask for permission to progress

Some trainers will tell you to start closing as soon as you start talking. They fondly describe it as ABC – Always Be Closing. I don't agree.

I believe what is likely to happen is that your customer will feel pressured into doing something they may not want to do, or are not yet ready to do.

But don't worry – there are some simple techniques you can use that really don't feel like pressurizing your customer at all.

The "Alternative Close"
A big favorite, and one of the easiest, is simply to offer an alternative:

"Which day is best for you to receive delivery – Tuesday or Friday?"

"Which distributor would you prefer to supply you, Smith's or Brown's?"

"We pack these in boxes of 24 or 48; which would be best for you?"

You are simply asking a question – and the answer is your order.

This may lead you into some form of negotiation but that's OK; if the customer is about to give you some commitment to buy, then negotiation is the right thing to happen at this stage.

Referred close

Use their competition

This is a simple technique that relies on the buyer's knowledge of his market and the other players within it.

By implying that a competitor of the prospect company is gaining significant benefits from buying your product, they will feel compelled to react. By imply, I don't mean to suggest something that is untrue; I simply mean that confidentiality dictates that you cannot divulge details of transactions between yourself and other parties. What you can do however, is explain that:

> *"Other companies in your sector have found that, by switching to our products (or service), they have managed to increase productivity by up to 27%".*

The benefit you state can be any that your proposition gives, but, as I have said before, financial benefits are almost always the strongest.

Use:

- cost savings

- waste reduction

- quality improvements

- gaining market share

- any others that are relevant and significant in your prospect's market sector

to convince your prospect that ordering from you would be the best possible move in their current situation.

Ramp up the pressure!

You can make this type of close even stronger if you can gain permission from your existing customers to use their name as a testimonial.

Then you really can put the pressure on to buy by explaining that, in effect, a competitor of theirs is stealing a march on them by "having a more productive manufacturing process as a result of using my product".

Beware

Of being caught in the trap of discussing price. Always refer to value, which includes performance and quality, rather than simply the physical product or service.

Empathy close

Show your understanding

Assuming that you have blueprinted properly in the early part of the sale, you will have a clear understanding of the issues that are important to your customer – either the company or the individual. Therefore, by taking one or more of those issues and wrapping it up in the form of a 'close' ,you can ensure that the benefits of doing business with you are clear.

Let's take an example of a retail outlet that currently buys from the largest supply company in the market. The situation is that, because the supplier is the largest, they have to use the largest vehicles to deliver such large volumes of stock to their broad customer base.

The problem this gives is that these large vehicles simply cannot get down the narrow service road behind the retail premises and, therefore, stops on the restricted parking area at the front of the store and the driver walks through the showroom with boxes of product.

This not only disrupts traffic flow immediately outside your premises but is an unwanted disturbance to your browsing customers, as the driver walks through the showroom, bumping his or her way past shelves and display stands with your delivery.

Because your delivery vehicles are smaller, they can access the rear of the premises, preventing the difficulties described above.

Your close, therefore, is "Because we understand the needs of our customers to make discreet deliveries that do not affect the normal trading conditions they have, we have designed our logistics around the use of smaller delivery vehicles and efficient delivery schedules.

"Would that suit you better and enable you to carry on serving your own customers without disruption?"

Surely the answer then has to be "Yes"?

Your personal close

Make it personal

The most important part of every element of the sales process is to appear relaxed and confident.

Having that air of confidence is perhaps even more important in this area of closing the sale. So why not make up your own closing techniques?

Think about what type of conversation suits your style the most. What style do you feel most comfortable with? Looking at a specific customer, what style or approach do you think the buyer will react most positively to?

Beware

Only make a deal by closing if you are sure you want it. "Revenue is for vanity; profit is for sanity". Make sure it's business you want to close.

Have the same attitude to the close as you have to the questioning techniques, for example, and see it as no more than a continuation of the conversation you have been having over an hour or two or maybe over several meetings.

Remember that people like to buy rather than be sold to, so your question about closing the deal is no more than you offering your buyer some help to make his buying decision.

129

Summary

- Be confident when faced with an objection you need to handle. You should view it as no more than a request for more information – at least until you know that there is more to it than that

- It is absolutely critical that you validate the objection before you start to handle it, just in case it isn't real. Some people will not always be honest with you about the reason they have refused your proposition, so validating ensures that you don't waste your time on bogus objections. By asking a simple question, you will ensure that you address the real objection and move back into getting the deal closed

- Use strong justification statements to handle objections effectively. These should contain evidence that will persuade the contact that their fears are unfounded. Use examples of success in similar applications or conditions as the contact's organization, where you can prove the value of your proposition

- When handling financial objections, don't fall into the trap of feeling compelled to justify the entire price/cost. You should simply focus on the gap between your financial position and that of your competition and demonstrate value to bridge that gap

9 Handling Objections

Hot tip

You must validate the objection BEFORE you handle it. Some people will be less than honest with you and, if you don't validate, you will spend time handling a false objection.

Objections are just questions

An objection is simply a reason your prospect or customer gives you not to purchase your product. Sometimes, admittedly, it's just an excuse, but sometimes there is a valid reason behind it.

In most circumstances, your prospect contact will be very upfront with you and simply tell you that they don't want to buy and they will tell you the reason why.

When this happens, you should not see it as a negative at this stage – it is much more positive to view it as no more than a request for more information.

If you receive an objection, it means that, so far, you haven't delivered adequate perceived benefits in your proposition to persuade your prospect to give you a positive response to your request for an order.

Be confident
The best way to approach an objection is with confidence.

Find out what the detail behind that objection is and then you have more information you can use to re-shape or simply re-state your proposal. Objections fall into two categories:

● Financial

● Non-financial.

They should be handled slightly differently, which is outlined in the diagrams that follow.

Validate it first
The very first thing you need to establish, when faced with an objection, is whether it is real or not. By that, I simply mean the prospect is saying no with one objection when there is actually a different issue that prevents them from proceeding with the order.

For example, if someone has a supplier they want to keep because they are entertained well by that supplier, it is very unlikely that they will admit that to you.

And nor should they – it simply demonstrates their lack of professionalism – but it happens.

...cont'd

To check the validity of an objection, you need to simply ask another question:

> *"If I can satisfy you on that specific issue, can we then proceed?"*

If the objection is real, they have to give you a positive response to that question. If they respond negatively, it means one of two things: either it wasn't real in the first place or they had more than one objection.

In that situation, once again, simply ask another question:

> *"What else is preventing us from moving forward with this proposal?"*

The prospect can now only give you the other objective or make up another false objective.

Once again, check the validity with the same question. If you need to, continue to go through this process until you eventually get a positive response to the validity question.

Uncover objections early

Another skill that will serve you well is having the ability to recognise an objection when the prospect offers it up in your conversational dialogue – your information gathering stage.

It is very likely that you will be given information in the answers to your questions that indicate an objection to your product or company without it being at the "close" stage of the Sales process.

As I said before, some people will be very up front and honest with you and simply say no when you ask for the order, but there will be other times during your conversation where a comment is made that is really an objection disguised in the form of a statement – make sure you really listen to what is being said so that you can recognize it and handle it.

Don't forget

You must be prepared to handle real objections with strong justification statements. An objection is effectively a plea for more information.

133

Hot tip

Look for what isn't said as well as what is. Often people will only tell you part of the truth and you have to seek out the rest before attempting to handle it.

Handling the real objection

Use evidence

To handle an objection, you need benefits as well as evidence to back them up and strengthen their power.

Once you have established that the reason given is a real issue for your customer, you have to find a way to minimize the strength of that objection.

Often, of course, an objection will be formed through lack of belief or confidence. You may have made a claim during your proposition that is simply unbelievable to the customer.

Using evidence from other customers, or from test and trial results, can prove your claim and convince the customer that their fears are unfounded.

The reason you need to handle financial objections slightly differently is very simple: a financial objection will be a concern over the "gap" between your value or cost against that of your competitor.

Therefore, avoid falling into the trap of handling the objection as the actual price of your offering – it's not. It is only that perceived gap that you need to handle.

Justification statements

Justify your position

Knowing the benefits you, your product or service, or your company can offer is just the starting point.

To handle objections effectively, you need to be able to present them in such a way that the recipient of the benefit really does get enough value, the proposition then becomes irresistible to them.

Given that these objections are often centered on a lack of belief and/or confidence, you need to present some evidence, in the form of a Justification Statement, that will allay those fears.

I mentioned tests and trials previously and these really can come into play in this situation.

You might like to practise using some of the following phrases to help handle the objections that have been put in the way of your next order:

Don't forget

You should only justify the gap in your perceived proposal, rather than the whole offer.

> *"In trials we carried out in our test centre, we have found that, typically, in applications exactly the same as yours, our product lasts twice as long as the product you currently use."*
>
> *"You probably know of (name of another company in the same sector) and they have found that, by switching the service provision to us, they have improved their productivity by 35%."*
>
> *"If you'd like to look at this results analysis, you will see that, against all of our major competitors, we come out top in terms of performance and value."*

Obviously, you will want to tailor these not only to your own offering but to your own style.

You need to be happy, confident and comfortable in making these statements and you will only be able to do that by doing so in a manner that suits your personal delivery style.

...cont'd

Confidence will get you through

At no time in the sales process is appearing confident more important that now.

The real benefit of that is simple; if you appear totally confident in your response to the objection given, the justification statement will carry so much more weight and you are then more likely to be believed as a result of it.

You only have to consider the way the stock market fluctuates based on confidence - or lack of it - in one particular sector or product.

Oil prices often rise because there is a 'fear' that a crisis or conflict in the oil-producing region will reduce supply. Before anything actually happens to restrict that supply, the prices start to rise simply through a lack of confidence.

The Objection Chain

Some people just seem to have that air of confidence, and, if you don't, you have to ensure that you find a way of at least appearing as if you do.

Often simply having total knowledge about your subject and the benefits will give you that confident aura.

It's also useful to have that library of testimonials and test results with you at all times, so you can refer to them and deliver the confident statement that will make the difference between success and failure.

Here is the process for handling both financial and non-financial objections:

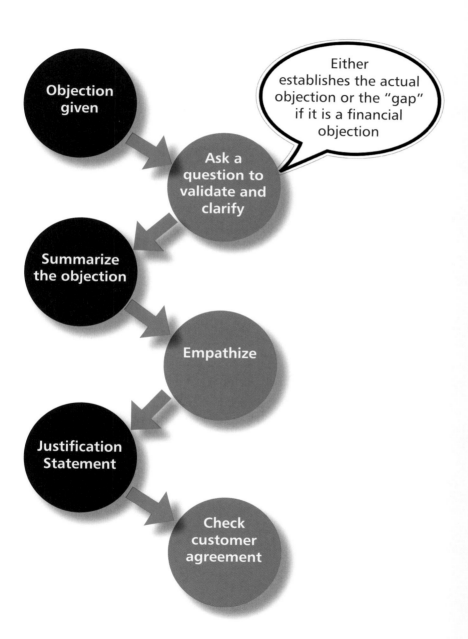

Summary

● Be confident when faced with an objection you need to handle. You should view it as no more than a request for more information – at least until you know that there is more to it than that

● It is absolutely critical that you validate the objection before you start to handle it, just in case it isn't real. Some people will not always be honest with you about the reason they have refused your proposition, so validating ensures that you don't waste your time on bogus objections. By asking a simple question, you will ensure that you address the real objection and move back into getting the deal closed

● Use strong justification statements to handle objections effectively. These should contain evidence that will persuade the contact that their fears are unfounded. Use examples of success in similar applications or conditions as the contact's organization, where you can prove the value of your proposition

● When handling financial objections, don't fall into the trap of feeling compelled to justify the entire price/cost. You should simply focus on the gap between your financial position and that of your competition and demonstrate value to bridge that gap

10 Negotiation

Definition

Negotiation : "To talk with others in order to reach an agreement"

Selling :   "To exchange for money"

Negotiation is the process of searching for an agreement that satisfies both parties. A real negotiation implies a win-win situation, in which all parties come away feeling content with the outcome.

Know the difference

Negotiating is not the same as selling, however, but most sales situations will, at some point, involve at least some negotiation.

Learning to become a successful negotiator will help you be successful in everything you do – both at work and at home. Because a successful negotiation will leave both parties feeling happy with the outcome, it is not going to be how much you can get out of your customer but more about what situation would leave both of you pleased with the prospect of doing business together. Remember that you are in this for the long-term relationship – not a quick hit never to be repeated. Negotiation is a vital part of the process and can be the key factor in determining how valuable the deal is.

Yet more preparation

Like every other element of the Sales process, your best results in a negotiation will be achieved if you have planned and prepared well. There are several factors you should consider before going into the negotiation, to ensure that the outcome is the most favorable it can be.

That preparation actually starts during the earlier stages of the sales process and can include issues like:

- Ensuring strong customised benefits during your proposition

- Handling objections credibly with convincing justification statements

- Not moving into negotiation too quickly

Don't forget

Don't negotiate too early. If you haven't gained at least a tacit agreement to do business, you shouldn't be conceding ground on any part of your proposition.

140

Don't forget

Think long term when negotiating.

Things to consider

Once you know that a negotiation is going to be necessary to move the process forward, you need to consider other issues in preparation for your discussion with your prospect:

- Who has the advantage? It's not always the customer

- Can you anticipate their position?

- Competitive positional strength?

- How are you perceived?

- Will you be setting any precedents and have there been any set in the past?

- What is your "breaking" point?

- What constants do you have that are non-negotiable?

- What concessions might you make and what is the "cost" to you and "value" to them?

- What value will the return concessions have to you?

- How will you justify the concessions you make?

- Possible customer negotiation points that could lead to deadlock?

- What previous negotiations have taken place and how could they influence this one?

- Are the levels of authority appropriate for the decisions to be made?

- What tactics might the customer employ?

Having well thought out plans for each element of the negotiation will create the opportunity to ensure that you truly do negotiate rather than concede.

Beware

Don't give concessions without knowing the true cost to your organization. If you get this piece wrong, you could end up agreeing to a position that later proves to be unattractive to you.

141

Negotiation versus selling

There is certainly confusion about whether negotiation and sales are the same. Let me put that to bed right now – the truth is, they are not.

You could put it simply by saying that sales is the process that allows the customer to buy something the supplier wants to sell.

Negotiation is the discussion around the terms under which that transaction takes place; specifically the detail, most of which will be commercial. Most sales people are trained in selling skills but, surprisingly, most are not given negotiation skills training.

For some reason, many companies leave that particular subject matter for senior managers.

Negotiate for profit

This situation not only surprises but truly alarms me because good negotiation techniques are a critical part of the process and can easily add 10% to sales revenues, and this goes straight to the bottom line as profit because it attracts no additional sales (or other) cost.

I'm going to spend more time on this topic than I have on some of the others, simply because I feel that it is so important and yet so few sales professionals have developed the edge in the negotiation element of agreeing a sale.

When to start negotiating

Negotiation should only start when both buyer and seller are conditionally committed to the sale (do not be drawn into negotiation before the principles of a sale agreement have been reached).

The prospect is very likely to attempt to bring the negotiation into play before the sale has been agreed. As I said before, the negotiation element of the sales process will have a fundamental affect on the attractiveness of the deal and is, therefore, vital to the financial results of the selling organization.

Negotiation generally results in a price compromise between seller and buyer, but don't restrict it to that element of the agreement – there are many other conditions that can be negotiated and will influence the attractiveness of the outcome. Therefore, under no circumstances whatsoever do you start the negotiation process before you have that initial agreement to do business.

If you are not sure if the customer is conditionally committed to the sale, ask a conditional closing question, such as:

"If we can agree the details, can we go ahead?"

If the answer is "no", you still have some selling to do. Once ground has been conceded, it cannot be regained and you will have immediately given the position of strength to the other person.

Take a collaborative approach

These days, the aim of negotiation should focus on collaboration rather than traditional confrontation, or a winner-takes-all result.

Although the temptation for most sales people is to create a winning result of the long-term benefit of the business relationship, the collaborative approach will yield the best overall results.

The ideal method is to think creatively and work in co-operation with the other side to achieve an outcome that will most benefit both parties.

...cont'd

By developing a partnership approach during the negotiation stage, you are already building trust and confidence in your business relationship. It should go without saying that you are looking to build a long-term relationship with your new found customer, so approaching this critical part of the sales process in the right way is vital.

A partnership approach entails both parties outlining the issues or conditions that are important to them and then doing everything they can to reach an agreement, where each side achieves as many of those conditions as possible.

Identifying concessions

From a sales perspective, once you have found out which issues are potential deal breakers for your customer, you have to do everything feasible to satisfy them.

The issues that are less important are much more likely to be conceded by each party. If all goes well, the critical issues for your customer will not be critical for you, so let the customer have them.

In turn, you can then take a more rigid stance on the critical issues for your own organization.

Make a note of the issues

As a starting point, it's a very good idea to write a list of the issues that are important to each side.

Remember to include both personal and emotional elements because these are just as important as commercial issues. The contents of that list represent a 'cost' to each party, either to give or to concede, and the individual costs will vary.

As part of your planning for the negotiation, you can evaluate the costs from your own perspective, which will then help you determine which aspects are more flexible than others.

Given that negotiations are often about finding that middle ground between two starting points, by offering one or more concessions from the customer's list, you can ask for some from your list to be agreed with in return.

Hot tip

Always put a value on the concessions you give. Only then are they likely to carry sufficient weight to influence the end result of the negotiation.

Who goes first?

Whoever makes the opening offer is undoubtedly at a disadvantage.

If you go first, the buyer can choose to disregard it and ask for a better offer. Also, this scenario means that the buyer avoids the risk of making an offer themselves that is more beneficial than you would have been prepared to accept.

It's amazing how often a buyer is prepared to pay more than the asking price, but avoids having to do so because they keep quiet and let the seller go first. Vice-versa, the seller can often achieve a higher selling price than he anticipates if he hears what the buyer is prepared to offer first.

The key, therefore, is to let the other side go first. Sometimes you will be pleasantly surprised at what the buyer expects to pay, which obviously enables you to adjust your aim. Letting the other side go first is a simple and effective tactic that is often overlooked.

After you!

Letting the buyer go first on price or cost also enables you to use another tactic, whereby you refuse to even accept the invitation to start negotiating, which you should do if the price or cost point is completely unacceptable.

For you to be able to do this, you must have previously planned for the negotiation and decided what your "break" point is. This then forces the other side to go again or at least re-think their expectations or stance, which can amount to a huge movement of momentum in your favor before you have even started.

However, if you cannot achieve more than your break point, then don't negotiate – simply walk away.

Don't forget

You must decide what your breaking point is before the negotiation process starts. If you reach that without agreement, you must walk away from the negotiation – you simply can't do business together.

Success is influenced by pressur

In your selling position, if you have lots of other potential customers, and, therefore, can walk away without fear of failure in your overall achievement of targets, the pressure is off you and the relaxed approach you can adopt is likely to bring you success.

On the other hand, if you are desperate for the sale, you are clearly much more likely to concede early and lose any advantage you may otherwise have been able to negotiate, and that can be that additional % revenue and profit.

The same will apply to your customer, of course, and that's exactly why many buyers will give you the impression that they can go somewhere else – even if they can't or don't want to. They know that this weak position gives you the advantage.

How to strengthen your position

This, therefore, means that, when you are in the sales position, the more you can create the impression that there is no alternative comparable supplier, the stronger your position.

You have to create the perception that your product or service is unique, and that the other person has nowhere else to go; he cannot afford to walk away. This positioning of uniqueness is the most important tactic, and it is one that comes into play before you even start to negotiate. Even if the product you are offering is not unique, remember that you are part of it. You can still create a unique position by the way you conduct yourself; build trust, rapport, and empathize with the other person.

Establishing a position (or impression) of uniqueness is the single most effective technique when you are selling, whereas denying and finding flaws in a product's uniqueness is the most powerful tactic the buyer can employ.

Always start high

Aim for your best outcome – a good buyer will always aim low and, given that they will always ask you to start the negotiating process, if you aim too low, you've lost ground immediately. Remember that your very first offer represents the absolute best outcome that you can achieve. It will never get better and almost always get worse. Conversely, that opening positioning of yours represents the minimum expectation of the customer.

If you remember that you can concede on issues other than price, you can afford to allow that opening position to be high because you may have already planned, through the creation of 'wish lists', what you can concede in other areas that still have a value for the buyer.

The psychology of negotiation

More often than not, negotiations come down to little more than finding the center ground between two starting points. The thing you must try to find is the other person's 'break point'.

Everyone has one and, once you know where that is, you can aim for your best outcome. It's also worth remembering that the easier the negotiation, the less satisfying it is.

Take, for example, your attempts to buy a house. The sale price is £250,000 and, after viewing, you put in an offer for £200,000, which is immediately accepted. How do you feel? I would guess that your immediate reaction would be delight, as you have managed to get what you want at a real knock-down price.

Then you sleep on it and wake up the next day feeling that the vendor dropped such a large amount of money so quickly that, actually, they would have been willing to drop even more.

Alternatively, if your offer of £200,000 was refused and the vendor then asked you to move nearer to the asking price and suggested £230,000, you might end up settling at £220,000. You have, therefore, paid 10% (£20,000) more than in the first scenario but, psychologically, you are likely to feel more satisfied with the eventual outcome. The same emotions will be present in your sales negotiation.

Help the other person if you can
Don't forget that your customer will have political issues to handle, too.

The quality of the outcome, from his or her perspective, may have a significant influence on his own position within his organization.

Several successful contract negotiations might be the key to a promotion or to an increase in salary. That buyer might have more to gain or lose than what just happens in your specific negotiation.

Once again, if you are aware of that, you can help by giving the right concessions to maximize his needs while minimizing the cost to you.

You should always seek return concessions when giving some of your own. This will ensure a balance and a truly fair finishing point.

Return concessions

Never give away a concession without getting something for it in return.

Depending on the approach taken by the customer, they may not want to offer anything at all. If that is the case, you are not in negotiation. You are simply in a situation where something has been offered to you at a very specific set of conditions and all you have to do is decide whether you want to accept it or not.

This is not an unusual stance for buyers to take and I would urge you to resist, if those demands are too high. Walk away and find a more reasonable (and, therefore, more profitable) customer.

Make them agree first

When positioning your request for a return concession, always put the priority on getting that concession first. Therefore, your language will be:

"If you can agree to ...., I will agree to........."

As with other suggested statements, it's perfectly reasonable for you to use your own language and style – simply ensure that you request before you offer.

Beware of setting precedents

If you start your trading relationship that way, no matter how long you do business together, that dynamic will always exist – give on your part and take on the customer's. The only time it might stop is if there is a change of personnel with the customer.

Keep the package together

A tactic often used by buyers is to attempt to break up the conditions of doing business into small chunks and gain an advantage in each one.

The chances are that, because they are smaller pieces, you might concede more easily because you are thinking of the end result, or at least you are thinking of the end result as it stood when this process started.

This could mean that, by the time you reach the end of negotiations, you realize that you have agreed to something that is different from what you thought initially. So that's why you need to keep the big picture in your mind at all times.

Note keeping

Make sure that you keep detailed notes as the negotiation proceeds.

You won't remember everything a day or two later, so it's vital to do it as you go. It also prevents either party from 'remembering it differently' further down the line.

As you will be making these notes as you go, you can also demonstrate that you are interpreting what has been agreed correctly by summarizing what you have written.

Also make sure that you give the customer a copy of these notes – both photocopied handwritten notes on the day and a follow-up of typed records of the discussion soon afterwards. (The sooner the better, while everything is still fresh in both party's minds).

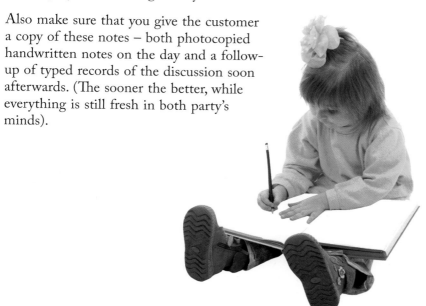

You cannot negotiate with someone who simply wants to win. Then you have to decide whether you want to concede for the sake of the business – or not.

Taking a tough decision

Be prepared to walk away...

If the break point your customer is adopting is just too demanding or not commercially viable, you must kill it there and then. Just come right out and say it:

> *"I just can't get to that position. If that is what it's going to take for us to trade, then I'm sorry to say I'll have to walk away."*

Of course, this might (and sometimes definitely will) lead to a breakdown and no business being conducted but it might also bring about a shift in position by your customer.

It really does depend on that pressure position – how much each of you wants to do business with the other.

Don't sell your soul – you will always regret it. Be brave enough, and strong enough, to walk away.

Potential customer tactics

I mentioned preparing for potential tactics used by your customer during the negotiation stage. Here are a few that are used, some more common than others:

- Either arranging for or allowing interruptions during the negotiation

- Bringing someone in part way through – this will always be someone more senior

- Aggressive atmosphere

- Distractions to put your off track

- Showing anger at not getting what they want

- Suggesting that they are bored with the process – either verbally or with their body language

- Running out of time, and therefore, putting pressure on you to "deal"

- Being very friendly to entice you to do them a favor

- Not giving all the points they want to negotiate

- Putting pressure on you by using phrases like:

> *"Just some minor details to finalise…"*
>
> *"It's looking good in principle…"*
>
> *"We're nearly there…"*
>
> *"Your competition is very keen…"*

- The nibble tactic – which means "nibbling away" at things you have already agreed to get a better deal (this can be done during or after the negotiation discussion)

- Devaluing your concessions

- Making you work hard

- Conceding on the easy issues

Beware

Don't allow the other party to nibble away at the agreed position. This can happen immediately after the conclusion or several days later. If you have reached a negotiated settlement, stick to it.

Beware

This is a Negotiation and not a strong-arm tactic by one side or the other. Your mutual goal should be to find a solution you are both happy to trade with.

.

Summary

- Negotiation is about reaching an agreement that both parties are happy with. It's the cliché "win-win" situation – although the reality is usually that one side wins just a little more than the other…

- You cannot negotiate with someone who doesn't want to negotiate an agreement. By definition, negotiation necessitates concessions given and taken, so a rigid negotiator won't move on their position and an agreed settlement can't take place unless you concede everything. If that happens, you have NOT negotiated

- You must plan well and ensure that you have prepared your benefits and justification statements, to use to strengthen your position

- Make sure you are aware of the mistakes you must avoid. Falling into well planned traps will immediately weaken your position

- Understand exactly which concessions you are prepared to give and calculate the "value" they represent to the customer

- Always get return concessions to compensate for the ones that you have given

- Be aware of what precedents you will be setting, which could make future negotiations more difficult

- Be ready for the tactics your customer might employ to help them achieve their desired outcome

- Never start negotiating until you have agreed, in principle, to do business together

- Don't go into a negotiation when you are under pressure for turnover – you will make subjective decisions that are unlikely to produce an inequitable outcome for you

- Be prepared to walk away from the negotiation, and potentially the business, if the demands of the customer are too great

11 Key Account Management

Don't forget

You can only Key Account Manage 3 or 4 customers per person. It is a time and resource consuming activity and spreading it too thin would eliminate the perceived gain delivered by adopting this strategy.

A brief outline

This chapter on Key Account Management is no more than an outline of:

- what it is

- the key elements of it

This method of selling strategy is complex and broad and needs a whole book to itself. I cover it here simply to give you an overview of what it is, as it is an inherent part of the sales process for some organizations.

An uncommon approach

The most surprising thing about Key Account Management is that so few people and companies adopt it as their default way of working.

It is my view that this approach should absolutely dominate the way every company thinks and plans its activity. It is so much more than a sales strategy – it's a company strategy.

It should dictate almost every element of how a company operates, and all decisions should refer back to the Key Account Management Plan. If the actions support the Key Account Management Plan, then go ahead; if they don't, then why are you doing them?

Most elements of Key Account Management are fundamental and easily identified. That's the good and bad part of Key Account Management. It's good because it's mostly common sense and structure. It's bad simply because so few people take advantage of the power of good key account management, and it is, therefore, often overlooked.

It's an organizational strategy

You need your company to behave in a way that supports rather than hinders you; it really is true to say that some organizations operate in such a way that selling becomes very difficult and strenuous.

Find out more

This is such a huge subject in itself, I merely want to give you an understanding of the basic principles so that you can consider adopting this method to grow your customer base, and the yield you will earn from it.

A definition

Key Account Management (KAM) is simply a way of operating so that you build:

1 strong

2 sustainable, and

3 mutually rewarding relationships

by working in a collaborative way, focusing every element of what you do on its relevance to that relationship.

In its purest sense, your organization will develop its Business Plan in support of KAM and, indeed, the organizational structure will be created to ensure the right people are in the right roles, doing the right things to optimize the relationship between supplier and customer.

Beware

Do not select those customers who are not prepared to work in partnership. If you do, the end result will be lots of giving by you and lots of taking by them.

How many accounts?

A chosen few

Considered wisdom suggests that any organization can only handle around 35 Key Accounts. The outer limits are 5-50, although somewhere in between would be more appropriate.

That means that you, as an individual, are likely to have no more than 2 or 3 Key Accounts.

The reason is simple – for a Key Account customer to get the attention and focus from the entire organization (not just the sales function) they need to grow disproportionately and they need that attention to be concentrated. You just can't do that if you are managing too many accounts.

There is plenty of evidence of organizations that have run a hugely successful Key Account Management programme with 30 accounts and then doubled that number with the belief that they will then be even more successful.

The reality is that the original list starts to fail due to the lack of focus, resources and attention. They become 'ordinary' merely through their number.

Knowledge is the key

It is absolutely impossible to create a strategic plan for your customers if you don't know enough about them.

Of course, if you don't know enough about your Partner customers, how can you empathize with them?

I have included a number of forms to help you identify the issues you need to have knowledge of in order to adopt a KAM programe.

By completing these information-gathering forms, you will put yourself, and, therefore, your company in a position to satisfy the needs of the customer and grow a strong relationship with them. Because it is a partnership approach, you can only do this with a customer who wants to be your partner.

It can't be forced and you may have to sell the benefits of the relationship as it will mean each company sharing sometimes potentially sensitive information with each other.

So trust and integrity is vital – one break in that trust and the whole relationship can fail.

157

Strength in contact

In any business relationship, the strength is not only determined by the quality of relationship, but quantity too.

The more people from each organization who know, communicate and trust each other, the stronger that relationship is and the more difficult it is to break (by a competitor).

The same principles apply as outlined in Chapter 4 – Building Relationships. You must ensure that you have several points of contact from each organization in regular communication with each other.

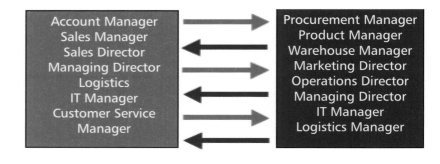

A partnership

KAM is fundamentally about a partnership approach.

It entails giving and receiving sometimes sensitive information and including the other party in the decision making, which will affect the relationship.

If one side tries to win or gain the upper hand against the other, it won't work – both sides must want mutual prosperity, and respect the need for profit generation and productivity improvements.

Take a look at the forms in the Resources chapter, which will give you the framework for starting a KAM approach and, if you are not already using this approach, why not make this a solid starting point to begin sustaining a strong, rewarding and enjoyable trading relationship?

Hot tip

Treat this as a partnership relationship by getting many contacts from both organizations talking to each other and building strong relationships.

Summary

- Key Account Management is a strategic approach used to manage activities and relationships within a few, carefully selected, critical customers. It should be adopted by the entire organization, not just the Sales team

- A KAM approach can only be adopted for a few carefully selected customers. This is not a "mass customer" approach because it is very resource intensive and should dictate the overall company strategy and direction

- Having considerable good quality information about those customers involved in your KAM program is vital, to ensure that you have a good understanding of the customer's needs, drivers, direction and future potential opportunities

- Have a broad contact surface to strengthen and maintain excellent relationships and to develop a Partnership approach. Safety in numbers really comes into play here, as, if one or two people from either company leave or change roles, the relationship can be maintained by those that remain

12 Exhibitions

A different sales approach

Although attending exhibitions may not be a regular or frequent part of your sales activity, it can be a vital source for sales leads and opportunities. The approach taken to maximize the opportunity they create is different. It is different because you will have a short period of time to question, build rapport with and convince those customers you meet that your offer is worth their further consideration.

This is only an outline of some of the key elements of Exhibition Selling, which I hope will steer you in the right direction to ensure a profitable return on the significant investments that exhibitions represent.

Ratios – again!

I talked earlier about the importance of knowing your ratios when planning your territory activity and it is just as important to carry out the same calculation here.

I am assuming that your organization will have decided what the primary objectives of the exhibition, are in terms of leads gained. To ensure your activity is at the right level, you need to ensure that your ratios relating to footfall are in line with that primary objective.

How many people to see?

Therefore, you need to estimate the average conversion rates of visitors to the stand to quality leads. This will ensure that you are in line for reaching your goals and it will also allow you to manage your resources.

If, for example, you need to have 100 leads per day from the stand and the exhibition is open for 7 hours, you will probably need 10 people in attendance at any given time.

My ratios for this example were:

Visitor to lead conversion rate:	4:1
Leads needed per day	100
Therefore, engaging conversations required	400
Average conversation per individual per hour	6
Number of conversations per hour needed	57
Number of people in attendance at any time	9.5

These are simply examples and you clearly need to calculate those conversions and ratios that fit your business and your typical performance.

Beware

Don't look busy and, therefore, uninviting. Avoid using your mobile phone or laptop, which gives the message of "do not disturb!"

Hot tip

Use friendly behavior to encourage visitors to step up to your stand. Engage them with an interesting "opener" to get them talking.

Encouraging visitors to your stand

Don't look too busy

The creation of your exhibition equipment and display will probably be outside of your control.

Typically, marketing will take care of that activity and the appropriate decisions, in conjunction with all internal interested parties.

Therefore, once the stand has been erected and equipped, it is down to the behavior and actions of those in attendance, which will directly influence the end result.

It goes without saying that you will want to make potential visitors feel welcome to step up to the stand and engage in conversation. Their motivation to do that will be affected in no small way by how comfortable they feel about crossing that line.

As well as being welcoming, you should be aware of the barriers you could unwittingly create, which will have the opposite effect. A fairly long list of behaviors you should avoid are listed below.

What not to do

- Eating on the stand

- Chatting to colleagues and, therefore, being preoccupied

- Texting or talking on your mobile phone

- Looking like a bunch of aggressive salespeople

- Appearing too formal and, therefore, not inviting

- Sitting down and appearing as if you don't want to be disturbed

- Nobody available

- Hunting in pairs

- Wandering aimlessly around your own stand looking bored and disinterested

- Closed body language

- Pouncing on visitors as soon as they step up to the stand

- Stuck on the stand – not getting into the traffic in the walkways

- Using your laptop and, therefore, making yourself unavailable

- Reading

- No other visitors at the stand

You have control over all of these issues, so ensure that neither you or your colleagues demonstrate these behaviors as they will lead to a lack of footfall wanting to come and talk to you to find out about your products and services, and therefore, potentially becoming leads for future business development.

Beware

Don't hunt in packs. Two or more people approaching a visitor is likely to be intimidating and will ensure a quick retreat from your potential new customer.

165

Don't forget

Get involved in the passing traffic. If you are not getting enough visitors, you need to get in the walk-ways to encourage more to cross that line.

Beware

Identify timewasters. Many people attend exhibitions purely for a day away from work or to collect give-aways. Be polite but move on to more productive visitors.

Getting visitors interested

Engage visitors quickly

For your exhibition, you need to create some powerful "hooks" as opening statements to make someone want to talk to you further.

Make sure you put some time and effort in well before the exhibition starts. Sit together as a team and decide what those hooks will be.

The good news is that most exhibition people don't do this. That gives you the opportunity to stand out from the crowd as being differentiated immediately, from the perceived quality of yourself and your colleagues.

Typical opening statements or questions I hear are:

> *"Are you OK there?"*
>
> *"Is there anything I can help you with?"*
>
> *"Are you having a good time at the exhibition?"*
>
> *"What does your company do?"*

Now, I'm quite sure that you don't need me to point out just how weak those are. They certainly wouldn't entice me to walk up to the stand and engage in conversation.

So yours need to be strong and contain a question where the answer to which will lead nicely into a conversation. An example could be along the lines of:

> *"Hello, my name is Gary Collins. Thank you for visiting our stand; tell me, what products are you interested in seeing at this exhibition?"*

Or:

> *"Hello, my name is Gary Collins. Thank you for visiting our stand; tell me, what, if anything, do you know about our products?"*

The answers to these questions will enable you to ask further questions and, without any fuss or bother, you are now in a conversation.

You can now engage in information gathering questions, as I outlined in Chapter 5, which will enable you to gauge whether this visitor represents a real, quality potential lead for future follow-up.

...cont'd

Just a short reminder that, if you have wandered into the walkways to entice people to visit the stand, you simply drop the "thank you for visiting our stand" part. It is obvious when you read it here, of course, but, when on auto-pilot as some of us are during these situations, it is very easy to trot out the same lines repeatedly, even when they are not appropriate.

If the information you get from these first few questions makes it obvious that the visitor is not going to fit your criteria for a quality lead, simply invite them to:

"Take a look around and come back to me or one of my colleagues if there is anything you need more information on."

That way you become free to seek out the next potential quality lead, ensuring that your exhibition objectives are met.

Other reminders

Everything that you need to do comes from the earlier chapters. Ensure that you remember to:

- Ask good quality consultative questions

- Demonstrate attentive listening skills

- Use summarizing to confirm your understanding

- Have your justification statements prepared to enable you to handle objections effectively

- Remember that your "close" in this environment is to get permission to make contact in the future, to progress the discussion on how your product or services could give customized benefits to the visitor's organization

- Follow those quality leads obtained QUICKLY!!! There is nothing sure to reduce interest in you and your company than untimely contact after an exhibition discussion. Before the exhibition starts, part of the panning process should be the allocation of sales resources to follow these leads up and make appointments for quality customer meetings

Hot tip

Having demonstrations on your stand creates interest. If your product is conducive to an impressive demonstration, make sure that there is enough space for a decent crowd to form.

167

Summary

- Recognize that you have a small window of opportunity to identify potential customers and gain commitment for a follow-up sales call. Be effective and efficient and don't waste time on those visitors who are unlikely to turn into future customers

- Ratios are even more important in exhibition selling, so ensure you have them calculated and then work them!

- Demonstrate behaviors that will encourage visitors to walk up to your stand so that you can engage them. This means making yourself approachable and interested

- Avoid those behaviors that suggest that you're too busy doing other things and, therefore, are unavailable to show products, answer questions and give information

- Create interest with demonstrations and exhibits with a "wow" factor, if possible

- Be prepared to get into the walkways to engage with exhibition visitors to encourage them to step onto your stand for a productive conversation

- Have great "hook" statements and good quality questions ready to gain the interest of visitors, so they are prepared to spend their time talking to your rather than visiting other exhibitors

- The usual rules apply regarding demonstrating excellent listening skills and engaging visitors. Make visitors feel that you are interested in them, their company and maybe their problems, with the aim of solving them

13 After Sales Service

"It is not the strongest of the species that survives, nor the most intelligent, but the one most responsive to change."

Charles Darwin

You've only just begun

Once you have taken that first order, you will naturally be delighted that all your hard work, skill and guile has paid off. And rightly so! This customer may have taken many months to convert.

However, it's critically important that you remember that the real work has only just started. That new customer is now a "Prospect" for your competitors, not least of which is the specific competitor that you have just wrestled this business away from. They will be attacking you in their attempts to win back the sales revenue they have just lost – exactly the same as you would.

Continue the good work

Part of your strategy for winning work was to identify the needs and wants of the customer and to satisfy them. You must ensure that you continue that process long after those early orders have been received. It will also be helpful and constructive to involve others within your own organization, to continue the good work.

Remember the Contact Surface Diagram on page 56, where I described how you should get as many people within each organization talking to each other to truly develop a strong and binding trading relationship. This is your chance to do exactly that, by lining up activities and contact on a regular basis to maintain, develop and grow the business you are now enjoying from your new customer.

Why you need to do this

If it's not obvious, I will briefly explain why this is such an important part of your customer process now that you have won this business, after investing large sums of your own company's money with prolonged sales activity. There's the first clue right there – to gain payback of the investment made!

Just think about what reaction you will get from your competitors now that THEIR business is in fact YOUR business.

1. They will attack you with increased firepower

2. They will probably offer a price reduction, to keep or regain the business

3. They will invest disproportionate resources to recover their losses

4. They will take it personally – as they should!

Now that you own this business, you become the target; you must respond positively to maintain what you have fought so hard for and you must demonstrate to your new customer exactly why they made an excellent decision when they chose to move their business to you.

Keeping up with change

One of the biggest issues we all face is change. All around us, changes frequently and with, what seems to me increasingly rapid pace. That change is caused by a number of factors and will typically fall into the following areas:

People changing roles
A new contact may have different needs and objectives. You need to quickly understand what these are and how you can satisfy them.

Market dynamics
Markets will shift through political, financial and competition influences. New players will increase the pressure on quality or price, or both, as they strive to gain a foot-hold into an already established market.

Economic
Boom or recession will unavoidably impact on volumes, quality, pricing and demands. They can and will be both positive and negative, depending on the economic conditions that prevail at the time, and you need to be ready to react positively. Being proactive is even better, by showing your customer and the market that you are Market Drivers not slow to respond laggard.

...cont'd

Technology

Ordering and stocking processes, in particular, are strongly affected by changes in technology. Increasingly, customers want to trade electronically and, without that capability, you risk being alienated and pushed out. In future, the likelihood is that almost all ordering, invoicing and payment will be made electronically. Technology is also delivering significant improvements in product quality and capability, which customers will not only enjoy but come to expect and demand.

Legislation

Often legislative change will be around Health & Safety policies but will also impact environmental policies and, potentially, customer expectations and demands – depending on what markets you operate within.

Political

Political change will inevitably lead to policy change – after all, that's what the new government has won its time office on. Be the first to discuss any significant changes in political policy that might impact your market or your customers. I am not suggesting having a political discussion with your customer contacts – in fact, I urge you not to have those conversations - they are fraught with danger, due to political persuasion! However, if a change in policy is going to alter operating conditions, your proactive approach will help secure long-term trading relationships.

Therefore, you need to have the skills and attitude to not only accept change but actually embrace it! It's coming whether you like it or not so you have a choice; fight against it (it's still going to happen!) or embrace it and adopt the style, attitude and behavior that will ensure that change works in your favor.

Of course, for us to effectively manage that change, we must be able to know what it is that is changing and, if possible, pre-empt that change so that we are not only ready but can be the first out of the blocks to demonstrate to our customer that we have our fingers on the pulse – we know what is happening in the world.

We all understand that technology is the fastest driver of change (Moore's Law states that the power of computers is doubling every 18 months) but other elements can and will cause the changes that we face regularly in our trading relationships.

Customer contact strategy

Something I have found to be hugely beneficial to both organizations is to have a Customer Contact Strategy. This simply means that you develop and agree a schedule of contact between the personnel of your own and your customer's organization, to maintain contact and handle day to day tasks. For example, if you have a Customer Service or Telesales function within your company, why not develop the operational relationship between those people and the relevant customer contact.

Agree that your colleague in Customer Service will call the buyer every Tuesday afternoon at 3:00pm. Naturally, you will organize the time and date, as well as the frequency, to match the needs and value of the customer organization. Some may need daily calls, others monthly or even quarterly. The more frequent the calls, the more strength the relationship will gain from this activity.

Day-to-day issues

The Customer Contact Strategy I have described above does more than just build and maintain the relationship: it allows those time-consuming issues to be handled by someone else, so that you can invest your valuable sales time in developing even more new customers, to deliver the sales growth that we all need.

Typically, the issues that can be handled this way include:

- Order taking

- Stock returns

- Complaint handling

- Progressing outstanding orders

- Invoice queries

- Communication of changes in terms and conditions

This strategy will undoubtedly improve the overall trading relationship between you and your customer, as well as freeing up your own time. It will truly add "value" to your new customer as well as differentiating you from the competition, who is trying to fight back!

It will ensure a rapid response to customer issues, as they have a direct point of contact, which most customers do put a value on. In my experience, what also happens is that the customer will prepare for the next call from Customer Service by having the relevant orders/queries/complaint information ready to hand so that they can be handled quickly and efficiently during that scheduled call. In fact, when I have offered to handle an issue face to face, I have often been told "No, that's OK Gary, I'll handle it with Liz when she calls!"

Other benefits from regular contact

There are many benefits from this regular customer contact, many of which I have already outlined. The good news is there are even more! Consider the ability of your competitors to break down the strong bond between you and your customer when you are regularly delivering excellent customer service with considerable "added-value". This activity will effectively mean that:

- The cost of change for your customer becomes very high

- The risk of change is increased

- The cost of entry for your competition has increased

- You have driven change in increased customer expectation and demand

- You will create customer loyalty through an outstanding customer service offer

- You will minimize customer loss to ensure you achieve your Sales growth targets

Making it happen

Clearly, a small amount of preparation is needed to set this contact strategy up and here are the simple steps to make it happen:

- Establish the capacity of your colleague for making customer calls

- Quantify that capacity in terms of number of calls per day/week/month

- Decide which customers would benefit most from this contact

- Discuss your plans at the next customer meeting, to gain their agreement

- Establish WITH the customer the frequency of calls and who would be best placed to receive those calls

- Communicate the agreed schedule to your Customer Service colleague and ensure the calls are scheduled

- Take the Customer Service contact to meet the customer at least once a year and at the very least within a few weeks of setting up this Customer Contact Strategy

- Review with both customer and colleague quarterly, to ensure frequency and content is appropriate and effective

- Ensure that you remind your customer on a regular basis what excellent added-value you are delivering through your after sales service and Customer Contact Strategy

Summary

- Winning new business is just the beginning of the hard work. Now you must ensure that you maintain it

- Developing good business relationships with new customers will allow your company to gain a pay-back for the costly Sales time you have had to invest in the process of conversion for a competitive account

- Develop a Customer Contact Strategy that will tighten the bond between the two trading organizations and keep competition at bay

- Free up your valuable and scarce Sales time by allocating day-to-day issues to a colleague

- Regularly review your Customer Contact Strategy to ensure its appropriateness and to remind your customer of the overall benefits he /she enjoys from your trading relationship

- Welcome change and use it in your favor. Be a driver of change in customer expectations to increase the cost of entry to all newcomers who want to wrestle your customers away from you

- Create "loyal" customers to make your business safe, so that all other new customers are delivering Sales growth rather than replacing lost business

Resources

Relationship Status

Account Manager:
Customer:

1. What type of relationship do you want – how would you describe it?

2. What type of relationship does your customer want?

How close are you to (1) above (%)? ....

How close are you to (2) above (%)? ....

What do you need to do to achieve (1)?

1. ....
2. ....
3. ....
4. ....
5. ....

What do you need to do to achieve (2)?

1. ....
2. ....
3. ....
4. ....
5. ....

How well do you know your Customer?

Score each element out of 10:

0 = not at all: 10 = couldn't be better

Do you know:	Score
Your key customer's products and how you add value to them?	
The customer's strategic plan?	
The customer's financial health (ratios etc.)?	
The customer's business processes (logistics, purchasing, production, etc.)?	
What the customer values/needs from its suppliers?	
Your product as a proportion of the customer's spending?	
Which of your competitors does the customer use; why and how it rates them?	
How much attributable (interface) costs should be allocated to your customer?	
The real profitability of the customer to you?	
How long it takes to make a profit on a major new customer?	
Total	
Score as a percentage %	

That's how much you know about your KEY customer…

SWOT Analysis

Customer: _____

Consider the key issues for each area of your customer/prospect

STRENGTHS

WEAKNESSES

OPPORTUNITIES

THREATS

Segmentation

Customer: _____

Consider the key issues for this customer resulting from the SWOT analysis.

Critical Success Factors

Critical Success Factor Action plan

Relationship Contact Surface

Account Manager: ....

Customer: ....

Supplier		Customer	
Name	Position	Name	Position

Key Account Management Check List

Score each element out of 10: 0 = not at all: 10 = couldn't be better

Have you...	Score
1. Categorized your customers?	
2. Matched your relationship with each customer type?	
3. Got an up-to-date copy of your customer's organizational chart?	
4. Got a good understanding of the relevance and authority of each contact within your customer?	
5. Got an understanding about how each contact feels about your company … and you?	
6. Looked at the overall picture and identified relationship gaps that need addressing?	
7. Got strong relationships with people who are really important, or are they with nice but less significant people?	
8. Got poor or weak relationships with people who are really important with your customer?	
9. Got good relationships across all functions of the customer?	
10. Got support from colleagues in the relevant functions to be part of the overall relationship with your customer?	
11. Got all levels in the customer covered or are you only concentrating on one level? You could be missing important people at Board level or retail assistant level.	
12. The ability and opportunity to solve glitches in the supplier/customer process?	
13. Helped improve your customer's margin?	
14. Become a good source of information for your customer regarding issues that are not easily available, i.e. market trends, research data, etc.?	
15. Offered them expert advice on something that is new or difficult for them?	
16. Delivered training to their staff to help them market your products more effectively?	
Total	

Score ..../160   As a percentage................%

You have now identified which areas of your Key Account Management you need to work on.

Key Account Management Activity

Account Manager: _____

Sector: _____

What major activities will you become involved in to ensure you adopt a Key Account Management approach?

Activity   **Target date**

1. ....

2. ....

3. ....

4. ....

5. ....

6. ....

7. ....

8. ....

9. ....

10. ....

How committed are you to make these activities happen? Circle one number...

1   2   3   4   5   6   7   8   9   10

(if you circle any number other than 10, you're actually not committed at all!)

Effective Customer Meetings

Company:

Who should be there:

Position

Position

Position

Purpose of meeting:

Primary Objective:

Secondary Objective:

What will make this a beneficial meeting from the CUSTOMER'S perspective?

What "HOOK STATEMENT" will I use to immediately engage the contact:

What OBJECTIONS might I receive?

What are my JUSTIFICATION STATEMENTS to manage those Objections?

190